Contents

Foreword

A decade has passed since the publication of the previous Government's policy on aviation in the Air Transport White Paper. Much has changed in that time. Passengers are benefiting from greater competition, with our busiest airports now in separate ownership and the aviation industry investing in upgraded airport facilities. The recession has knocked economic growth prospects and resulted in new trends, such as airlines increasingly consolidating their long-haul routes to a small number of dominant continental hubs. Other new 'global hubs' in the Gulf such as Dubai now offer good connections to larger airports around the UK. The EU Emissions Trading system and introduction of UK carbon budgets has changed the policy context on climate change.

But some of the challenges we faced in 2003 remain. For example, the need to balance the benefits aviation brings against its local impacts, such as noise. Both sides of the debate feel strongly about this.

On the question of airport capacity, the Government has now established the independent Airports Commission, led by Sir Howard Davies. The Commission is examining the nature, scale and timing of any requirement for additional capacity to maintain the UK's global hub status. The Aviation Policy Framework is an important piece in the jigsaw, setting out the principles which the Commission will take into account in working up its recommendations as it reports later this year and in 2015.

History shows that we need an agreed policy everyone can stick to before we try to act. Our aim is to achieve this through the Aviation Policy Framework and the work of the independent Airports Commission. While the Commission is considering the need for and location of any new airport to relieve the South East, I set out here a policy framework to support and challenge our airports right across the UK. Since taking up my post, I have emphasised the importance of all our national airports. They are more than regional or secondary centres.

The role of Government has also changed in the past decade. The 2003 Air Transport White Paper set out in detail which specific developments would be supported at particular airports across the UK. The Aviation Policy Framework does not seek to do this. It sets out the Government's objectives and principles to guide plans and decisions at the local and regional level, to the extent that it is relevant to that area.

The Government believes that aviation needs to grow, delivering the benefits essential to our economic wellbeing, whilst respecting the environment and protecting quality of life. The way ahead will be challenging as we work together to strike the right balance. But it is critical that we do so in order to safeguard our long-term economic prosperity.

The Rt Hon Patrick McLoughlin MP
Secretary of State for Transport

Aviation key facts

Aviation's contribution to the economy

- The aviation sector contributes around £18 billion per annum of economic output to the UK economy
- It employs around 220,000 workers directly and supports many more.

We are well connected now

- The UK has the third largest aviation network in the world, after the USA and China
- The number of passengers using non-London airports has increased by over a third since 2000
- London is currently extremely well connected and delivers the connections UK PLC requires with at least weekly connections to over 360 destinations. In comparison, Paris serves around 300 destinations and Frankfurt around 250
- The UK maintains its position as an attractive place to invest through London's position as a global city:
- 75% of Fortune 500 companies have offices in London
- In 2012, Aon, the world's largest insurance broker, announced it would move its head office from Chicago to London and Harvey Nash announced its decision to retain London as its global headquarters after considering Zurich and New York.

The future capacity challenge

- Our major airports face a medium- and longer-term capacity and connectivity challenge which the Government must tackle:
- Heathrow is operating to its capacity today
- Gatwick is forecast to be full in the 2020s and Stansted, which today has considerable spare capacity, is forecast to be full by the early 2030s.
- The Airports Commission will publish its interim report by the end of 2013 and its final report by summer 2015.

Tackling climate change

- The 'gross' emissions from aviation are forecast to increase between now and 2050 at both the UK and global levels
- However, under the EU Emissions Trading System (EU ETS), the 'net' emissions from flights covered by the EU ETS cannot increase above the level of the emissions cap
- Between 2013 and 2020, the annual emissions cap applied to the aviation sector within the EU ETS will be 95% of the average annual emissions between 2004 and 2006.

Aircraft noise

- The UK was instrumental in the agreeing a decision by the Committee on Aviation Environmental Protection (CAEP) within ICAO which requires new types of large civil aircraft, from 2017, to be at least 7dB quieter on average in total, across the three test points, than the current standard. Standards for smaller aircraft will be similarly reduced in 2020.

Executive summary

A balanced approach to securing the benefits of aviation

1. In July 2012, the Government consulted on its strategy for aviation: the draft Aviation Policy Framework. This proposed a high-level strategy setting out our overall objectives for aviation and the policies we will use to achieve those objectives. This final Aviation Policy Framework will fully replace the 2003 Air Transport White Paper as Government's policy on aviation, alongside any decisions Government makes following the recommendations of the independent Airports Commission.

2. The Airports Commission was established in September 2012 with the remit of recommending how the UK can maintain its status as a global aviation hub and maintain our excellent international connectivity for generations to come, as well as making best use of our existing capacity in the shorter term. By defining Government's objectives and policies on the impacts of aviation, the Aviation Policy Framework sets out the parameters within which the Airports Commission will work.

3. The Aviation Policy Framework has been informed by the 600-plus responses we received to our 2011 scoping document and the nearly 500 responses received to the 2012 consultation on the draft Aviation Policy Framework. It is underpinned by two core principles:

   - Collaboration: By working together with industry, regulators, experts, local communities and others at all levels, we believe we will be better able to identify workable solutions to the challenges and share the benefits of aviation in a fairer way than in the past.

   - Transparency: To facilitate improved collaboration, it is crucial to have clear and independent information and processes in place. Those involved in and affected by aviation need to have a clearer understanding of the facts and the confidence that proportionate action will be taken at the international, national or local level.

4. The main elements of our Aviation Policy Framework are summarised below and covered in more detail in the individual chapters.

The benefits of aviation

5. The Government's primary objective is to achieve long-term economic growth. The aviation sector is a major contributor to the economy and we support its growth within a framework which maintains a balance between the benefits of aviation and its costs, particularly its contribution to climate change and noise. It is equally important that the aviation industry has confidence that the framework is sufficiently stable to underpin long-term planning and investment in aircraft and infrastructure.

6. Chapter 1 of this document summarises aviation's benefits, particularly in helping to deliver connectivity. The UK is an outward-looking nation: an island economy that for centuries has owed its prosperity to the transport and trade routes linking it with the rest of the world. With the increasing globalisation of our economy and society, the future of the UK will continue to be shaped by the effectiveness of its international transport networks.

7. Aviation benefits the UK economy through its direct contribution to gross domestic product (GDP) and employment, and by facilitating trade and investment, manufacturing supply chains, skills development and tourism. The whole UK aviation sector's turnover in 2011 was around £53 billion and it generated around £18 billion of economic output.[1] The sector employs around 220,000 workers directly and supports many more indirectly. The UK has the second largest aircraft manufacturing industry in the world after the USA and will benefit economically from growth in employment and exports from future aviation growth. Aviation also brings many wider benefits to society and individuals, including travel for leisure and visiting family and friends.

8. Aviation in the UK is largely privatised and operates in a competitive international market. The Government supports competition as an effective way to meet the interests of air passengers and other users. We also welcome the continued significant levels of private sector investment in airport infrastructure across the country and the establishment of new routes to developed and emerging markets. For example, Vietnam Airlines' launch of their service to Hanoi and Ho Chi Minh City from Gatwick in December 2011 represented a new connection for London and a China Southern service between Heathrow and Guangzhou began in June 2012; the first-ever connection between these two airports. These are very important developments which clearly show that there is potential for UK airports to attract new routes.

9. **One of our main objectives is to ensure that the UK's air links continue to make it one of the best connected countries in the world. This includes increasing our links to emerging markets so**

---

1   Turnover, economic output (GVA) and employment figures are from Annual Business Survey, ONS, 2011 (provisional), Section H: Transport and Storage, adding SIC 51 (air transport), SIC 52.23 (service activities incidental to air transportation), SIC 30.3 (Manufacture of air and spacecraft and related machinery) and SIC 33.16 (Repair and maintenance of aircraft and spacecraft).

that the UK can compete successfully for economic growth opportunities. To achieve this objective, we believe that it is essential both to maintain the UK's aviation hub capability and develop links from airports which provide point-to-point services (i.e. carrying few or no transfer passengers). This should be done in a balanced way, consistent with the high-level policies set out in this document and acknowledging Government's commitment to economic growth.

10.   In the short to medium term, a key priority is to work with the aviation industry and other stakeholders to make better use of existing runway capacity at all UK airports. We are pursuing a suite of measures to improve performance, resilience and the passenger experience; encourage new routes and services; support airports in Northern Ireland, Scotland, Wales and across England; and ensure that airports are better integrated into our wider transport network.

11.   In the medium and long term beyond 2020 we recognise that there will be a capacity challenge at all of the biggest airports in the South East of England. There is broad consensus on the importance of maintaining the UK's excellent connectivity over the long term, but currently no consensus on how best to do this. A robust and generally agreed evidence base is needed before a decision can be made on the scale and timing of any requirement for additional capacity to maintain the UK's position as Europe's most important aviation hub. This is why Government established the Airports Commission in 2012.

Managing aviation's environmental impacts

12.   Aviation's environmental impacts are both global (climate change) and local (primarily noise, as well as air pollution and surface access traffic congestion). Chapter 2 covers aviation's climate change impacts. **Our objective is to ensure that the aviation sector makes a significant and cost-effective contribution towards reducing global emissions.**

13.   Aviation is an international sector, and global action to address a global challenge is therefore essential if we are to achieve progress on reducing its climate change impacts while *minimising the risk of putting UK businesses at a competitive disadvantage*. National governments have a particularly important role in pushing for effective international action. We are committed to making progress through the International Civil Aviation Organization (ICAO), the agency of the United Nations which regulates international civil aviation, on a global emissions deal and more stringent technology standards. We also continue to work with our European Union (EU) partners to ensure the success of the inclusion of aviation in the EU Emissions Trading System (ETS).

14.   In the absence of an ambitious global agreement to tackle aviation emissions, our strategy is to continue to strongly support action at a

European level. The inclusion of aviation in the EU ETS is a key component of this, and we remain committed to ensuring that the EU ETS is a success.

15. At the national level, the Government and industry are taking a number of actions to support the effective working of the EU ETS and help reduce international emissions, including airspace management and encouraging advances in lower carbon technology.

16. Chapter 3 covers noise and other local environmental impacts. The Government recognises that noise is the primary concern of local communities near airports and we take its impact seriously.

17. **Our overall objective on noise is to limit and where possible reduce the number of people in the UK significantly affected by aircraft noise.** The document makes clear that the acceptability of growth in aviation depends to a large extent on the industry continuing to tackle its noise impact and confirms that the Government expects the industry at all levels to continue to address noise. We recognise that the manufacturing industry across Europe has committed to ambitious long-term goals to reduce aviation emissions to one-quarter of 2000 levels by 2050 and to halve perceived aviation noise. To achieve this, we want to incentivise noise reduction and mitigation, and we also want to encourage better engagement between airports and local communities and greater transparency to facilitate an informed debate.

18. The Government's intention is that the Aviation Policy Framework should support sustainable development and be delivered in a way which is consistent with its principles.[2] Government's vision for sustainable development was published in February 2011.[3] This means making the necessary decisions now to realise our vision of stimulating economic growth and tackling the deficit, maximising wellbeing and protecting our environment, without negatively impacting on the ability of future generations to do the same.

19. For aviation's other local environmental impacts, such as air pollution, our overall objective is to ensure appropriate health protection by focusing on meeting relevant legal obligations.

20. Those who live closest to airports bear a particular burden of the costs, but also benefits, such as employment and convenient access to air travel. We therefore want to strengthen the arrangements for involving communities near airports in decisions which affect them. Chapter 4 focuses on the theme of working in partnership, particularly at a local level. It covers airport consultative committees (ACCs), airport master plans and airport transport forums (ATFs). **Our objective is to encourage the aviation industry and local stakeholders to strengthen and streamline the way in which they work together.**

---

2 http://www.defra.gov.uk/publications/2011/03/25/securing-the-future-pb10589/
3 http://sd.defra.gov.uk/documents/mainstreaming-sustainable-development.pdf

Role of the Airports Commission

21. History demonstrates that it will be easier to deliver a lasting aviation solution that is right for the UK with a generally agreed evidence base and a degree of political consensus. This is why we have asked Sir Howard Davies to lead a rigorous, independent review of all the options. The Airports Commission will examine the scale and timing of any requirements for additional capacity to maintain the UK's position as Europe's most important aviation hub and identify and evaluate how any need for additional capacity should be met in the short, medium and long term.

22. The Commission will provide an interim report to the Government by the end of 2013 setting out its assessment of the evidence on the nature, scale and timing of steps needed to maintain the UK's global hub status and its recommendations for immediate actions to improve the use of existing runway capacity in the next five years – consistent with credible long-term options. Its assessments of potential immediate actions should take into account their economic, social and environmental costs and benefits, and their operational deliverability. It should also be informed by an initial high-level assessment of the credible long-term options which merit further detailed development.

23. The Commission will then publish by the summer of 2015 a final report, containing:

    - its assessment of the options for meeting the UK's international connectivity needs, including their economic, social and environmental impact;

    - its recommendation(s) for the optimum approach to meeting any need;

    - its recommendation(s) for ensuring that any need is met as expeditiously as practicable within the required timescale; and

    - materials to support the Government in preparing a National Policy Statement to accelerate the resolution of any future planning application(s).

24. The challenge of maintaining the UK's international connectivity for future generations is a complex and contentious one, but solving it will be crucial to securing our long-term economic growth. On 1 February 2013, the Airports Commission published its first documents, which have begun the Commission's dialogue with interested organisations and the public: a guidance document inviting people to notify an intention to develop proposals and a discussion paper on demand forecasting. We encourage a wide spectrum of people to engage with this important and independent work.

Other aviation objectives

25. This Aviation Policy Framework focuses on the benefits of aviation and its environmental impacts, as responses to the scoping document and draft Aviation Policy Framework consultation confirmed that these were the priority areas that needed to be addressed. There are other important high-level policy objectives. Although they are not the subject of this Framework, they support and are consistent with it and are being taken forward separately. These objectives are summarised below.

Protecting passengers' rights

26. The Government is committed to improving the passenger experience, and the Aviation Policy Framework refers to actions we are taking to do this, for example through investing in surface access to airports and improving the border experience. When there is disruption at airports, it is important that passengers' rights are protected. Airlines have obligations under European law to ensure passenger welfare, and the CAA is working to achieve routine compliance with passenger rights. Good communication with passengers is also important at times of disruption.

Competition and regulation policy

27. We believe that the role of the Government should be largely confined to facilitating a competitive aviation market within a proportionate international and domestic regulatory framework to ensure a level playing field and the maintenance of high standards of safety and security. We will continue to work with the EU and ICAO on regulatory proposals to promote and protect UK interests.

28. Reducing the number of rules and regulations in our national life is central to the Coalition Government's vision for Britain, removing barriers to economic growth and increasing individual freedoms. The Government is committed to seeking alternatives to simply creating new regulations, as these often end up creating burdens and costs which affect businesses. Regulation should therefore no longer be the default response to addressing problems which arise. Our policies will be consistent with this approach.

29. The Civil Aviation Act 2012 modernises the economic regulatory regime for airports overseen by the Civil Aviation Authority (CAA). Present and future passengers and owners of cargo will be placed at the heart of the regulatory regime, with the CAA's current four equal duties being replaced with a single primary duty to further the interests of users of air transport services. Furthermore, the inflexible system of fixed five-year price controls will be replaced with a licensing system, facilitating targeted and proportionate regulation. The Act also gives the CAA duties to publish or require others to publish information about airline and airport performance as well as the environmental effects of aviation. In addition, the Act confers certain aviation security functions on the CAA, and allows reform of the Air

Travel Organisers' Licensing (ATOL) scheme to provide greater clarity for consumers and a more consistent regulatory framework for businesses.

Airspace

30. The Government remains a strong supporter of the Single European Sky (SES) initiative, which has the potential to deliver real benefits by minimising air traffic delays, reducing aircraft fuel consumption and lowering the amount of emissions produced by the aviation sector. We also support the implementation of the CAA's Future Airspace Strategy (FAS),[4] which sets out the long-term vision on how we should change our airspace within the overall aim of modernising the UK's airspace system in the context of the SES objectives. The implementation of the FAS can also play a significant role in delivering our economic and environmental objectives in relation to aviation. For example, by improving the overall efficiency of our airspace we can also at the same time provide significant opportunities to minimise aircraft emissions and air traffic delays.

Safety

31. Air transport is one of the safest forms of travel and the UK is a world leader in aviation safety. Maintaining and improving that record, while ensuring that regulation is proportionate and cost-effective, remains of primary importance to the UK. Since 2003, rules and standards for aviation safety in Europe have increasingly been set by the European Aviation Safety Agency (EASA). The UK will continue to work closely with EASA to ensure that a high and uniform level of civil aviation safety is maintained across Europe. In 2009, the UK was one of the first countries to publish a State Safety Programme, in line with new ICAO standards. The CAA published its own Safety Plan[5] in 2011 outlining the additional action it will be taking to improve UK aviation safety performance.

Security

32. The threat to UK aviation remains high. To keep pace with the rapidly changing nature of the threat, the Government is seeking to move to an outcome-focused, risk-based regime for aviation security regulation in the future. To facilitate this the Government is working with industry to develop and roll out the implementation of Security Management Systems (SeMS), modelled on the safety management systems (SMS) approach already in widespread use by the aviation industry and its safety regulators. We believe this will provide even better aviation security by enabling more responsive and flexible approaches to new and emerging threats. In the future, it should also provide the industry with greater scope for innovation and efficiency in delivering security processes, potentially enabling security outcomes to be delivered in more passenger-friendly way.

---

4   *Future Airspace Strategy*, CAA, June 2011, http://www.caa.co.uk/docs/2065/20110630FAS.pdf
5   *Safety Plan 2011-2013*, CAA, 2011, http://www.caa.co.uk/docs/978/CAA_Safety_Plan_2011.pdf

Developing the Aviation Policy Framework

33. In preparing the Aviation Policy Framework, the Government sought views on a scoping document published in 2011 and consulted on a draft of this document in July 2012. The results of this consultative process have informed the policy set out here, and a summary of responses to the draft Aviation Policy Framework consultation is published alongside this document. We have also published some associated commentary in relation to particular areas where there was contention or a modification of our approach in the light of responses. Readers of both the consultative and final documents will see that many sections of the Framework are similar or the same. We are grateful to everyone who has taken the time to engage with the development of the Aviation Policy Framework.

1. Supporting growth and the benefits of aviation

Aviation's contribution to the UK economy

1.1   The UK has always been an outward-looking nation – an island economy that for centuries has owed its prosperity to the transport and trade routes linking it with the rest of the world. With the increasing globalisation of our economy and society, the future of the UK will undoubtedly continue to be shaped by the effectiveness of its international transport networks.

1.2   We believe that aviation infrastructure plays an important role in contributing to economic growth through the connectivity it helps deliver. For example, it provides better access to markets, enhances communications and business interactions, facilitates trade and investment and improves business efficiency through time savings, reduced costs and improved reliability for business travellers and air freight operations.

1.3   There is broad agreement that aviation benefits the UK economy, both at a national and a regional level. While views differ on the exact value of this benefit, depending on the assumptions and definitions used, responses to both the scoping document and the consultation demonstrated that the economic benefits are significant, particularly those benefits resulting from the connectivity provided by aviation. In addition we believe there to be social and cultural benefits from aviation. This chapter summarises the main benefits of aviation.

Gross domestic product and jobs

1.4   The air transport sector's turnover is around £28 billion, and the sector directly generates around £10 billion of economic output. It provides about 120,000 jobs in the UK and supports many more indirectly.[6] These figures do not include the aerospace sector, which is covered below.

1.5   The economic importance of the aviation sector extends beyond its direct contribution to UK Gross Domestic Product (GDP) and employment, as an enabler of activity in many other sectors of the economy. These include

---

6   Turnover, economic output (GVA) and employment figures are from *Annual Business Survey*, ONS, 2011 (provisional), Section H: Transport and Storage, adding SIC 51 (air transport) and SIC 52.23 (service activities incidental to air transportation).

business services and also financial services where the UK enjoys a significant comparative advantage. The financial services industry requires on average six times as much air travel as some other sectors.

Imports and exports

1.6 Although air freight carries a small proportion of UK trade by weight, it is particularly important for supporting export-led growth in sectors where the goods are of high value or time critical. Air freight is a key element of the supply chain in the advanced manufacturing sector in which the UK is looking to build competitive strength. Goods worth £116 billion are shipped by air between the UK and non-EU countries, representing 35% of the UK's extra-EU trade by value.[7] [8]

1.7 The express air freight sector alone contributed £2.3 billion to UK GDP in 2010, and facilitates £11 billion of UK exports a year. Over 38,000 people are directly employed in the express industry, which supports more than 43,000 jobs in other sectors of the economy.[9]

1.8 A successful and diverse economy will drive a need for quicker air freight. Key components to keep factories working are often brought in from specialist companies in North America and the Far East. To keep production lines rolling this often has to be done at short notice. Access to such services is crucial to keeping UK manufacturing competitive in the global marketplace.

Manufacturing, skills and technology

1.9 The UK has the second largest aerospace manufacturing industry in the world and the largest in Europe. The growth prospects for the UK industry are sizeable based on global traffic growth predictions (£352 billion revenue up to 2030).

1.10 The UK aerospace industry is a key part of our advanced manufacturing sector, contributing towards rebalancing the economy to become less dependent on financial services. The UK has the second biggest aerospace industry in the world in terms of turnover, and is one of only a few countries involved in the design, development, manufacture and maintenance of the full range of aircraft products. The sector has an annual turnover of around £24 billion[10] of which 70% is exported.[11] It directly employs around 100,000 highly skilled workers and supports many more jobs indirectly.[12]

1.11 New and emerging technologies, such as unmanned aerial vehicles (UAVs), offer significant opportunities in the civil aviation field, for example in oil, gas

7 *CHIEF Non-EU data*, HMRC, 2011 (provisional data), https://www.uktradeinfo.com

8 *Trade statistics,* HMRC, 2011, https://www.uktradeinfo.com/Statistics/Pages/Statistics.aspx

9 Oxford Economics (2011) – The Economic Impact of Express Carriers in Europe – Country Report: United Kingdom

10 *UK Aerospace Industry Survey,* Aerospace, Defence, Security Trade Association (ADS), 2010
http://www.adsgroup.org.uk/pages/07003420.asp

11 *Ibid.*

12 Direct employment figure comes from ADS survey (http://www.adsgroup.org.uk/pages/07003420.asp.

and mineral exploration, air freight, search and rescue, data gathering and scientific research, as well as opportunities for technology transfer to the wider aviation sector.

Value of business and general aviation

1.12 The business and general aviation (GA) is important to the UK. Its contribution to the economy has been estimated at £1.4 billion per annum.[13] The sector delivers vital services, including search and rescue, mail delivery, life-saving (organ) transport, law enforcement, aerial survey and environmental protection flights, as well as underpinning the training of future pilots, ground-based aircraft engineers and technicians. The sector also covers a wide range of activities, from corporate business jets and commercial helicopter operations through to recreational flying in small private aircraft, including gliders. A Civil Aviation Authority (CAA)-initiated and chaired strategic review of the sector has acknowledged its growing economic importance, particularly for the British and European manufacturing industry

Greater productivity and growth

1.13 The UK's aviation sector enables productivity and growth in the following ways:

- enhanced access to markets and new business opportunities through improved connectivity;

- lower transport costs and quicker deliveries. For example, transporting freight by air allows smaller inventory holdings, and the rapid transport of perishable goods leads to increased specialisation of production which results in greater efficacies. The Organisation for Economic Co-operation and Development (OECD) notes that 40% of international freight trade by value is accounted for by airlines;[14] and

- facilitating inward investment and the movement of goods, people and ideas both within the UK and to and from the rest of the world thus enhancing trade and the diffusion of knowledge and innovation.

1.14 Some of the main benefits to consumers and businesses from greater investment and effective use of airport infrastructure include:

- reductions in delays and disruption[15] as a result of airport congestion, which affect airlines, passengers and the wider community;[16]

---

13 *Strategic Review of General Aviation,* CAA, 2006. Estimated at approximately £1.4 billion in 2005

14 According to Steer, Davies, Gleave (2010) in 2008, goods worth £95 billion were shipped by air freight between the UK and non-EU countries, representing 35% of the UK's extra-EU trade. Heathrow is the dominant gateway, with 63% of UK air freight volumes and, for non-EU trade, 63% of UK air freight value, the vast majority of which is carried in the belly hold of passenger aircraft. Heathrow is also the largest UK port by value for non-EU trade, with 24% of the total, similar to the combined total for the country's two principal container ports, Felixstowe and Southampton.

15 There would also be resilience benefits as there would be more spare capacity to help recover from any problems (e.g. snow) thus leading to fewer cancelled flights.

16 *Economic Survey of the United Kingdom,* OECD, 2009, http://www.oecd.org/document/18/0,3343,en_2649_33733_43092599_1_1_1_1,00.html

- increased frequency and range of flights to faster-growing economies.

Tourism

1.15   Air travel is essential to the *Government Tourism Policy,*[17] which aims to attract four million extra visitors to England alone over the next four years. China and other emerging economies will be a major source. Similarly ambitious targets have been set by other parts of the UK to increase their number of visitors. Good connectivity from the UK to emerging economies is likely to increase the scope for growth in inbound tourism from these countries in future. Overseas residents made 31 million visits to the UK in 2011, with nearly three-quarters of these visitors arriving by air. Earnings from overseas visits were £18 billion, 84% of which was spent by people who arrived by air.[18]

1.16   Consultation responses were divided on the economic impacts of outbound tourism. Some respondents considered that there was a 'tourism deficit', as more UK residents travelled abroad than overseas residents travelled to the UK. Other respondents highlighted that outbound tourism supports UK-based jobs in the travel and airline industry and boosts high street consumer demand before trips are made. The latter has been valued at around £27 billion per year.[19] Responses confirmed that the 'tourism deficit' question is a complex one and that the evidence available to us does not show that a decrease in the number of UK residents flying abroad for their holidays would have an overall benefit for the UK economy. UK residents made 57 million visits abroad in 2011 and spent £32 billion, 84% of which was spent by residents who travelled abroad by air.[20] The Government believes that the chance to fly abroad also offers quality of life benefits including educational and skills development. Overall the Government believes continuing to make UK tourism more attractive is a better approach both for residents and attracting new visitors.

Travel, culture and family

1.17   In addition to its economic contribution, aviation provides wider social benefits, enabling UK citizens to experience different cultures or enjoy a well-earned holiday. In an increasingly globalised society visiting friends and relatives is an increasingly important reason for flying; for example in 2011 it was the most common purpose of travel at Heathrow (36% of trips), Stansted (45%) and Luton (43%).[21] Visiting friends and relatives also forms a significant proportion of business for airports outside London and the South East, which in some cases helps maintains the viability of their air links.

---

17   *Government Tourism Policy*, DCMS, March 2011,
      http://www.culture.gov.uk/images/publications/Government2_Tourism_Policy_2011.pdf

18   http://www.ons.gov.uk/ons/rel/ott/travel-trends/2011/rpt-travel-trends-2011.html

19   *The UK Tourism Satellite Account*, ONS, 2008, http://www.ons.gov.uk/ons/rel/tourism/tourism-satellite-account/2008-
      --the-economic-importance-of-tourism/uk-tsa-2008.pdf

20   http://www.ons.gov.uk/ons/rel/ott/travel-trends/2011/rpt-travel-trends-2011.html

21   *CAA Passenger Survey 2011*, http://www.caa.co.uk/default.aspx?catid=80&pagetype=90

1.18 The UK's extensive historical links with many parts of the world and our resulting multi-cultural society will continue to drive a high demand for visiting friends and relatives air travel. For example, the consultation has highlighted the efforts of British Asian communities to secure and encourage further services from airports such as Birmingham, Manchester and Leeds-Bradford to various airports in India and Pakistan.

1.19 During the consultation the Government heard evidence about the wider cultural and societal benefits of travel. While this is hard to quantify numerically the Government found the case persuasive. The continued popularity of overseas travel highlights a resilient appetite for travel among the British people.

Supporting airports across the UK

The growth and importance of airports outside London

1.20 One of the Government's aims in helping the economy to grow is to encourage investment and exports as a route to a more balanced economy. Airports are in some ways cities in themselves, creating local jobs and fuelling opportunities for economic rebalancing in their wider region or area. New or more frequent international connections attract business activity, boosting the economy of the region and providing new opportunities and better access to new markets for existing businesses.

1.21 The Government recognises the very important role airports across the UK play in providing domestic and international connections and the vital contribution they can make to the growth of regional economies. For more remote parts of the UK, aviation is not a luxury, but provides vital connectivity. Nineteen million passengers took domestic flights in 2011.[22]

1.22 Many airports act as focal points for business development and employment by providing rapid delivery of products by air and convenient access to international markets. For example, Birmingham Airport employs only 500 people directly, but 150 companies on the airport site employ a total of 7,000 people.[23] East Midlands Airport acts as a hub for freight, with three of the four global express air freight providers and Royal Mail maintaining major operations from the site.

1.23 Airports in Northern Ireland, Scotland, Wales and outside the South East of England also have an important role in helping to accommodate wider forecast growth in demand for aviation in the UK, which could help take some pressure off London's main airports. The availability of direct air services locally from these airports can reduce the need for air passengers and freight to travel long distances to reach larger UK airports.

---

22 *CAA airport statistics*, 2011, http://www.caa.co.uk/docs/80/airport_data/2011Annual/Table_10_2_Domestic_Terminal_Pax_Traffic_2011.pdf

23 More information is available on Birmingham Airport's website at: http://www.birminghamairport.co.uk/meta/careers/vacancies.aspx

Airports outside the South East

Airports outside the South East are vital to their local and the national economy, and many are growing and creating jobs. For example:

Aberdeen Airport supports some 3,870 jobs and contributes around £126 million every year for the Scottish and UK economy. Based on current levels of employment and the predicted passenger growth forecasts, an additional 1,110 jobs are expected to be created, generating an additional £42 million Gross Value Added (GVA) for the Scottish and UK economy per annum. Businesses in the area rely heavily on the global connections provided by Aberdeen Airport – 56% of its passengers are business travellers, the highest rate of any Scottish airport.

Birmingham Airport is the UK's seventh busiest, with some 40 airlines operating scheduled services to over 140 destinations, including in the US, Caribbean and Middle East. The airport's central location and excellent surface links, combined with its ongoing programme to develop more long-haul services, will help boost the West Midlands economy and help ease capacity constraints as well as congestion at South East airports.

Bristol Airport currently handles approximately 6 million passengers per year and is the fifth largest outside London. Over 100 destinations across 30 countries are served by direct flights, including 13 European capital cities.

Approximately 2,700 staff, employed by over 50 organisations, work at the airport site. The airport plays a vital role in the economic success of the South West region, with its ongoing development projected to create additional income of between £1.9 and £2.0 billion.

Leeds Bradford International Airport is a vital contributor to the economy of the Yorkshire and Humber region, and in particular the Leeds City region. Currently the airport supports up to 2,800 direct jobs and generates GVA of £102.6 million in direct value. In addition, it acts as a catalyst to a further 320 jobs and £10.8 million of GVA. The services of the airport and international connectivity will continue to contribute towards improved export activity, performance and business competitiveness. Based on forecast passenger growth at the airport, it is estimated that this will grow to around 8,000 jobs and £290 million GVA by 2030

Manchester International Airport is the UK's fourth busiest airport, and busiest outside the South East, handling 19 million passengers in 2011 in its three terminals. Over 60 airlines currently offer direct flights to over 200 destinations. The airport's dedicated World Freight Centre handles around 150,000 tonnes of air freight per year, expected to increase to 250,000 tonnes per year by 2015. Around 19,000 people are directly employed at the airport. The airport owner's, Manchester Airport Group's, airports and property business contributes more than £3 billion to the UK economy and supports over 86,000 jobs. The airport is the site of the £650 million Airport City project at Manchester Airport – a mixed-used development that forms the central core of the newly designated Manchester Airport Enterprise Zone and will deliver 5 million square feet of new business accommodation over the next 10–15 years.

1.24   The Government wants to see the best use of existing airport capacity. We support the growth of airports in Northern Ireland, Scotland, Wales and airports outside the South East of England. However, we recognise that the development of airports can have negative as well as positive local impacts, including on noise levels. We therefore consider that proposals for expansion at these airports should be judged on their individual merits, taking careful account of all relevant considerations, particularly economic and environmental impacts.

Responses by airports

Airports are already responding to local demands. For example:

- Birmingham Airport has recently completed a terminal development project that will enable the airport to cater for 18 million passengers (compared with the approximately 9 million handled to date per year) and is taking forward plans for a runway extension. This will allow the airport to handle larger aircraft flying to more long-haul destinations from 2014, which will maximise regional opportunities and help meet additional UK demand.

- Southend Airport has completed a programme of investment that has transformed the airport. A new terminal has been constructed, a runway extension that allows the operation of newer-generation, high-efficiency, medium-capacity aircraft has been completed, and an airport railway station that offers direct rail links to London opened in September 2011. As a result, Southend Airport expected to handle one million passengers in 2012 and create 500 new jobs.

- Leeds-Bradford Airport recently completed a £11 million development of its passenger terminal. This has created a 65% increase in airside space over two floors in the terminal.

- In addition, ongoing investment programmes at other airports such as Bristol, Manchester, Newcastle, Glasgow, Edinburgh, Belfast City and Belfast International are delivering additional improvements to airport capacity, airport facilities and the passenger experience.

Air connectivity to London

1.25   A number of respondents to the consultation – particularly from Scotland, Northern Ireland and some English regions – stressed strongly that continued connectivity to London airports is essential to their regional economies and to national cohesion. This was highlighted by the 2012 sale of bmi and its associated domestic services.

1.26 We fully recognise the importance of air services to these areas, and will be inclined to support applications by devolved and regional bodies to establish Public Service Obligations (PSOs) that comply with the specific PSO conditions within EU law,[24] where necessary to protect services between other UK airports and London.

1.27 The Devolved Administration, or Local Enterprise Partnership (LEP) or local authority in England, will continue to be responsible for developing the business, financial and legal cases required by the EU regulation on PSOs, and for demonstrating the importance of particular air services to the economic development of areas of the UK. The Department for Transport would need to be reimbursed for any funds provided for subsidies, should these be required.

1.28 Establishing a PSO would enable airport slots used for that service to be ring-fenced so that an airline could not use them for a different route. Importantly, however, the current EU slot allocation regime stipulates that PSOs should be justified by economic need, which is more likely to be based around linking cities and regions, rather than specific airports. This means that, when judging whether a UK region has adequate air services to London, it would be necessary to take into account the level and nature of services to all five of London's main airports.

1.29 We acknowledge concerns expressed by some respondents that increasing capacity constraints at Heathrow have diminished access for domestic air services. Air links between some UK airports and Heathrow have ceased. However, many still have air links to other London airports, as well as links to intercontinental aviation networks through services to mainland European and other international hubs. There is no longer a direct air service between Heathrow and Inverness Airport, but Inverness has direct connections to Gatwick and Luton and has gained connections to Amsterdam Schiphol.

Route Development Funds

1.30 Route Development Funds (RDFs) – a form of EU state aid – have previously supported the establishment of some new air services from airports in the UK. These included services supported by the Welsh Assembly Government from 2005 and the former North East Regional Development Agency from 2006. However, changes to the EU Aviation State Aid Guidelines,[25] which came into force in autumn 2005, have significantly reduced the scope for RDF support.

1.31 The 2005 guidelines impose significant restrictions on the levels of financial support and types of service that could be supported through RDFs. Essentially, they limit state aid to intra-EU services serving smaller airports

---

24 European Parliament regulation of 24 September 2008 on common rules for the operation of air services in the Community *(1008/2008)*, http://eur-lex.europa.eu/LexUriServ/LexUriServ.do?uri=OJ:L:2008:293:0003:0020:EN:PDF

25 Communication from the Commission: Community Guidelines on Financing of Airports and Start-Up Aid to Airlines Departing from Regional Airports (2005/C 312/01). The guidelines were published in the Official Journal of the European Unions on 9 December 2005.

and regions with low passenger demand, and mean that long-haul routes and services from larger airports outside the South East can no longer be supported.

1.32   We recognise that the provision of start-up aid for new air services from airports outside the South East helps significantly towards improving connectivity and economic growth. The UK has highlighted to the European Commission concerns that the current guidance on start-up aid does not provide sufficient scope to support the establishment of routes from outer regions of the EU, including routes from within Northern Ireland, Scotland and Wales. We will continue to press for more flexibility in the application of start-up aid that will help with the establishment of new services at airports outside the South East, where such aid would not distort competition

Extending regional liberalisation policy

1.33   For many years, the Government has sought to open up access to the airports outside the South East to improve opportunities for connectivity and to help reduce demand on South East airports. In the late 1990s the Government adopted an explicit open access policy, whereby other countries were offered, on a reciprocal basis, unrestricted access to airports in Northern Ireland, Scotland, Wales and regional airports in England, and in exchange UK airlines would have unrestricted access from these airports to those of the other country.

1.34   There is no evidence to suggest that the UK's current bilateral air service arrangements are presenting a significant constraint on either existing or potential services to UK airports outside the South East. Furthermore, many airports find themselves reliant on UK airlines to provide key access to important domestic and international destinations. Nevertheless, the Government believes that it would send a strong positive signal and increase competition to provide connectivity and further incentivise the launch of such services if the UK went a stage further and adopted a unilateral regional open access policy on a case-by-case basis. We are proposing, therefore, to offer bilateral partners open access to airports outside the South East in order to facilitate inward investment in new routes and extra choice for business and passengers without necessarily having to secure reciprocal access for UK airlines to the airports of the other country.

1.35   The granting of such rights would be subject to a case-by-case consideration within the context of the current position in the UK's bilateral aviation relationship with the country concerned (for example, we might not grant such rights if there were concerns that there was not a level competitive playing field in the market, such as if it were argued that the airline in question was in receipt of state aid that was distorting competition).

Connectivity

1.36 As explained earlier, aviation significantly benefits the UK because it provides us with excellent access to the rest of the world and brings us closer together within the UK. With the increasing globalisation of our economy and society, the future of the UK will undoubtedly continue to be shaped by the effectiveness of its international transport networks.

1.37 In summary, aviation connectivity is a combination of destinations served and frequency of flights: the broader the range of destinations served and the higher the frequency of flights to and from those destinations, the better connected an airport, city or country is. The value of connectivity is affected by other characteristics, such as the relative importance of the destinations served, the cost of accessing them, which is the end-to-end journey time and cost including the price of air travel, and the reliability of the services.

1.38 Hub airports play an important role in providing international connectivity, especially to long-haul destinations including emerging economies. Although there is no single agreed definition of a hub airport, a key characteristic of hub airports across the world is that they are able to serve more destinations and have higher frequencies than other airports. This is because a hub airport supplements local demand[26] with transfer[27] passengers, providing traffic volumes which support higher frequencies of services on more popular routes, and enabling services on more marginal routes that would not otherwise have proved viable with fewer passengers.

1.39 Excellent connectivity helps sustain clusters of specialised high-value industries in the UK such as the financial, legal, IT consultancy and business management sectors which are knowledge intensive and increasingly global in operations.[28] People in these industries travel widely in the course of their business and account for nearly a quarter of all aviation business travel.[29] However, businesses across a much wider range of industries – including chemical, oil, manufacturing and engineering, construction, retail, education, health, media, leisure, catering and transportation – use aviation to travel to service clients, to manage satellite operations and local offices, to source or sell business or manufacturing inputs and outputs and for overseas or multi-national companies based in the UK to reach global headquarters and other business partners.

---

26 Local demand refers to all passengers terminating their air journey at an airport, i.e. not connecting passengers.

27 Transfer passengers are passengers who connect directly between an inbound and an outbound flight, usually within 24 hours.

28 *Aviation Services and the City – 2011 update*, City of London Corporation, January 2011 http://217.154.230.218/NR/rdonlyres/63094787-5540-47BA-B2BC-2278674218D7/0/BC_RS_Aviation2011update.pdf

29 They accounted for 23% of all business passengers that listed a type of business in the 2010 CAA passenger survey.

The UK's connectivity today

1.40 The UK is currently one of the best connected countries in the world. We are directly connected to over 360 international destinations. Only China's and the USA's aviation networks are more extensive than the UK's, and Germany and France are in fifth and eighth place respectively (based on available airline seat kilometres[30]).[31]

1.41 The demand for aviation in the UK is concentrated in the South East, a densely populated region whose economy comprises multiplehigh-value sectors including finance, professional services, technology, media and fashion. This drives consistently high demand for aviation in the region, so that the five main South Eastern airports (Heathrow, Gatwick, Stansted, Luton and London City) account for nearly two-thirds of passengers at UK airports and nearly half of all air transport movements.

1.42 London is an exceptionally well served capital city: its five airports together serve more routes than any other European city.[32] Heathrow and Gatwick dominate the UK's long-haul market, accounting for 87% of direct passenger flights from the UK to North America, 99% to Brazil, Russia, India and China (BRIC) countries and 78% to the rest of the world (outside Europe).[33]

1.43 Heathrow Airport, as the UK's only international hub airport, has a unique role in supporting the UK's and London's connectivity. In 2011, Heathrow handled nearly a quarter of all air transport movements at UK airports, approximately a third of all terminal passengers and two-thirds of all air freight, which is mainly transported in passenger aircraft. Its service patterns tend to reflect trade patterns as well as passenger demand – see Figure 1.1.

---

30 DfT analysis of CAA statistics. Based on international destinations with at least 52 direct passenger flight departures (i.e. at least a direct weekly service) from at least one UK airport in 2011.

31 *Global Competiveness Report*, World Economic Forum, 2011-12, http://reports.weforum.org/global-competitiveness-2011-2012. Based on available seat kilometres, which is the number of available seats multiplied by the number of kilometres flown.

32 *Aviation Policy for the Consumer* (page 18, Figure 6: CAA analysis of OAG data), CAA, 2011, http://www.caa.co.uk/docs/589/CAA_InsightNote1_Aviation_Policy_For_The_Consumer.pdf

33 DfT analysis of CAA statistics, 2011

Figure 1.1: Value of UK services exported to foreign countries and the number of seats available from Heathrow, 2011

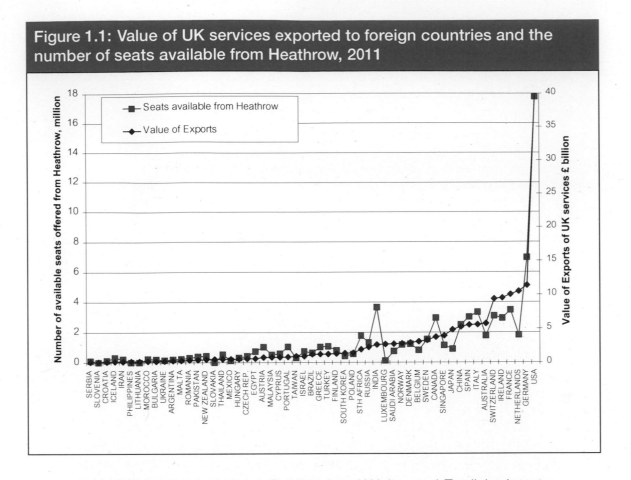

1.44 Airports in Northern Ireland, Scotland and Wales and English airports outside London also play a very important role in UK connectivity. As well as operating a range of domestic routes, many of which are important for business travellers, they serve an increasing number of routes to mainland Europe. In 2011, nearly 150 destinations in mainland Europe were served by at least one airport outside the South East. Although the long-haul market still accounts for only a small proportion of traffic at airports in Northern Ireland, Scotland, Wales and regional airports in England (3% of passenger flights in 2011), many now serve a number of long-haul routes. Over 35 destinations outside Europe have a regular service from at least one airport outside the South East;[34] these are mostly traditional holiday destinations in countries such as Egypt, North America, Morocco and Tunisia but a number of airports outside the South East also offer flights to major world cities such as New York, Dubai, Islamabad and Toronto. Most of these airports also enjoy connectivity to another EU hub airport.

1.45 In 2011, UK airports facilitated air travel for around 50 million business passengers[35] and provided direct access to over 360 international destinations. In addition to passengers, goods worth £115 billion were

---

34   DfT analysis of CAA statistics, 2011

35   Throughout this document numbers of passengers refers to the Civil Aviation Authority (CAA) definition of a ''terminal passenger' – a person joining or leaving an aircraft including passengers transferring between two flights. A transfer passenger is counted twice at an airport: once when leaving the first aircraft and then again when joining the connecting service.

shipped by air freight between the UK and non-EU countries.[36] Although air freight carries a small proportion of UK trade by weight, it accounted for 35% of the UK's extra-EU trade in 2011 by value.[37] It is particularly important for supporting export-led growth in sectors where the goods are of high value or time critical. Air freight is a key element of the supply chain in the advanced manufacturing sector in which the UK is looking to build competitive strength.

Connectivity in the future

1.46 The UK's continued economic success depends on being able to connect with the countries and locations that are of most benefit to our economy. This is important in relation both to destinations that fall into that category today and those locations that will become crucial to our country's economic success in the future. While it remains vital for the UK to maintain its connectivity with established markets such as the USA and in Europe, it is also important that we take advantage of the growing opportunities presented in the emerging economies of the world to remain competitive in the global economy.

1.47 There has been some increase in direct services from the UK to leading emerging economies over the last decade: the total number of flights to BRIC countries more than doubled over this period.[38] In 2011 Heathrow served 11 destinations in Brazil, Russia, India and China with at least a daily service, which compares favourably with all the major EU hubs. It also had more flights in total to BRICs than the other four main European hubs (Charles de Gaulle, Frankfurt, Madrid and Schiphol), with particularly strong connections to India and Hong Kong.

1.48 In the future the number of destinations served from Heathrow may continue to fall. The recent trend at Heathrow has been for profitable routes to be operated at higher frequencies, to meet the demands of business travellers; however, as Heathrow is constrained, airlines have had to reduce the total number of destinations they serve. Heathrow went from 175 destinations in 2006 to 157 destinations in 2010.[39] We will be monitoring this trend with a view to understanding what may happen at other airports as capacity becomes ever more constrained, and what the impact on connectivity will be.

1.49 There remains considerable scope for airports other than Heathrow to develop long-haul services to a broader range of destinations to support the UK's international connectivity, primarily through growing point-to-point services or connections to overseas hubs.

---

36 CHIEF Non-EU data, HMRC, 2011 provisional https://www.uktradeinfo.com/index.cfm?&hasFlashPlayer=true
37 Ibid.
38 DfT analysis of CAA statistics, 2011
39 From 165 destinations in 2002 and a high point of 175 destinations in 2006 to 157 destinations in 2010 (CAA statistics) destinations served at least weekly (at least 52 passenger flights during the year).

Aviation demand forecasts

1.50   In January 2013 the Department published revised aviation forecasts to inform a range of long-term strategic aviation policy issues including the development of this Aviation Policy Framework and the work of the Airports Commission.

1.51   These forecasts adopt the latest projections for the key drivers of aviation demand including economic growth from the Office of Budget Responsibility (OBR) and oil prices from the Department for Energy and Climate Change (DECC).

1.52   The central forecasts of passenger numbers in 2030 have been reduced by around 7% from levels forecast in August 2011. Primarily this reflects revisions from the OBR's forecasts for the UK economy and changed projections of oil prices from DECC.

1.53   Demand for air travel is forecast to increase at a slower rate than we have seen over the last 40 years, reflecting the anticipation of market maturity across different passenger markets and a projected end to the long-term decline in average fares seen in the last two decades. So whereas in the past we saw annual growth of 5% in the future it is likely to be between 1% and 3% over the next 15 years.

1.54   In the most likely scenarios the major South East airports are forecast to be full by 2030. However, other scenarios have this occurring as soon as 2025 or as late as 2040, depending primarily on the rate of economic growth and the price of oil.

1.55   According to the most likely scenarios a number of non-London airports, including Birmingham, Bristol, East Midlands and Manchester Airport, are also assessed as reaching capacity over a similar time scale.

1.56   Heathrow had effectively reached its maximum capacity in 2011 and it is forecast to remain at full capacity across all the demand cases considered.[40]

Conclusion

1.57   One of our main aviation objectives is **to ensure that the UK's air links continue to make it one of the best connected countries in the world. This includes increasing our links to emerging markets so that the UK can compete successfully for economic growth opportunities**. To achieve this objective, we recognise the importance of both maintaining the UK's aviation hub capability and developing links from airports which provide point-to-point services (i.e. carrying very few or no transfer passengers). This must be done in a way consistent with the high-level policies set out in this document.

---

40   The full forecasts can be found at: https://www.gov.uk/government/publications/uk-aviation-forecasts-2013

1.58 This Policy Framework seeks to achieve this objective, with a clear strategy for the immediate future, which is set out below. However the Government is committed to achieving this objective into the long term. Any decision the Government makes on airport capacity will be highly contentious. It is for this reason that we find ourselves again confronting issues that have been under discussion since the early 1990s. The Government is determined that our successors 20 years hence will not still find themselves in this position.

1.59 The Government set up the Airports Commission in recognition of the need to establish a solid independent evidence base for a long-term strategy. We have asked Sir Howard Davies to present an interim report by the end of 2013 on immediate actions to improve the use of runway capacity. But securing the UK's economic competitiveness, including by supporting London's status as a centre of global trade, requires a longer-term approach

Strategy for a vibrant aviation sector: the short term

1.60 In the short term, to around 2020, a key priority for Government is to continue to work with the aviation industry and other stakeholders to make better use of existing runways at all UK airports. Taking into account responses to the scoping document, our strategy is based on a suite of measures focused on:

- making best use of existing capacity to improve performance, resilience and the passenger experience;

- encouraging new routes and services;

- supporting airports outside the South East to grow and develop new routes; and

- better integrating airports into the wider transport network.

Improving performance, resilience and the passenger experience

Trial of operational freedoms

1.61 In 2011 the South East Airports Taskforce (SEAT) identified ways to make the most of existing airport infrastructure and improve conditions for all users at the three main London airports.[41] The key recommendations were on improving punctuality, resilience, and delay. In February, the airport operator completed a phased, 12-month trial of operational freedoms at Heathrow involving the more flexible use of its runways and departure routes. The purpose of the trial was to explore whether such measures could help to maintain the schedule, mitigate disruption and deliver a net environmental benefit through reduced stacking and by cutting the number of unscheduled flights during the night period. The trial was overseen by the

---

41 *South East Airports Taskforce Report*, DfT, 2011, http://www.dft.gov.uk/publications/south-east-airports-taskforce/

CAA and further information, including data from the trial, can be found on Heathrow Airport Limited's website.[42]

1.62 The Government will consult on the results of the trial later in the year before any decision is taken on whether to make these changes permanent.

Ending the Cranford agreement

1.63 To further improve operations and resilience at Heathrow we confirmed the ending of the Cranford agreement.[43] This is an informal but long-standing agreement not to use the northern runway for departures when the wind was in from the east (roughly 30% of the time). This decision needs to be implemented by Heathrow Airport Ltd and a planning application will shortly be submitted for the necessary changes to airport infrastructure. Following implementation, noise will be distributed more fairly around the airport, extending the benefits of runway alternation to communities under the flight paths during periods of easterly winds, and delivering operational benefits by letting the airport operate consistently whether there are easterly or westerly winds.

Airport performance charters and capacity utilisation guidelines

1.64 The CAA investigated the SEAT's recommendations on airport-specific performance charters and capacity utilisation guidelines through a CAA-chaired industry working group called the Airport Performance Facilitation Group (APFG). The purpose of the charters is to help motivate an airport's stakeholders to take decisions based on the interests of the whole airport system by setting out the level of service that airlines and their passengers should expect to receive.

1.65 In addition, airports were directed to look at the feasibility of developing guidelines that might optimise the utilisation of runway resource at each airport. For example, in 2012 the Heathrow airport community agreed to a winter schedule with some lower hourly capacity limits in order to improve reliability. Over time this will reduce the peak hourly pressure on the airport and thus strengthen resilience.

1.66 The work of the APFG concluded at the end of 2012, with further progress in these areas expected through the CAA's new powers to place the passenger at the heart of airport regulation under the Civil Aviation Act and their interaction with the Airports Commission.

1.67 In terms of making the best use of capacity at our busiest airports, particularly Heathrow, the Government supports in principle any reasonable, non-discriminatory steps that airport operators may wish to take to limit access to smaller aircraft, where appropriate. Such measures could help our busiest airports to maximise passenger throughput.

42 *Operational Freedoms Trial*, BAA, 2012,
http://www.heathrowairport.com/noise/noise-in-your-area/operational-freedoms-trial
43 *Theresa Villiers written ministerial statement*, 7 Sept 2010, http://www.publications.parliament.uk/pa/cm201011/cmhansrd/cm100907/wmstext/100907m0001.htm

US pre-clearance

1.68 Outside of the EU, the US remains the single most popular market for air services from the UK, with some 17 million terminal passengers at a number of UK airports flying to and from the US.[44] The US authorities provide immigration, customs and agricultural pre-clearance facilities at 15 airports outside the US,[45] including at Dublin and Shannon Airports in Ireland. These facilities, operated by US Customs and Border Protection (CBP), allow passengers travelling to the US to clear US arrival checks before departure, allowing for easier and quicker connections and arrivals in the US.

1.69 The Government believes that introducing US pre-clearance at the UK airports could offer significant passenger benefits and improve the overall end-to-end journey experience for passengers flying from the UK to the US, whilst at the same time maintaining passenger security and a secure border, which are shared US and UK priorities. The decision on whether to operate such facilities at airports overseas ultimately rests with the US authorities.

1.70 Accordingly, the Government will consider, with the US authorities and interested stakeholders in the UK, the feasibility of such facilities being made available in the UK, including the practical and legal issues that would need to be addressed.

Border controls

1.71 The Government also remains committed to working with the US authorities to take forward access for UK nationals to Global Entry,[46] the US's kiosk-based international registered traveller system that allows its participants to take advantage of expedited immigration clearance on arrival in the US. The UK's own registered traveller scheme – which will supersede the existing iris recognition immigration system (IRIS)[47] – is due to be rolled out from Spring 2013, and we are making good progress with the aviation industry to improve the provision of fast-track clearance at airports through a new premium service offering, as well as in improving both the coverage and availability of e-gates for clearing UK and European Economic Area (EEA) passengers who hold a biometric passport and are over the age of 18.

1.72 Building on the work done by SEAT, we are committed to working to improve efficiency at the border, to minimise queues, increase automation and to improve the passenger experience so that we achieve the best possible experience for people visiting or returning to the UK, whilst at the same time maintaining our border security. All of this demonstrates that the UK is open for business, and nothing underpins that more than maintaining safe and secure borders. Stringent checks at our borders are imperative if

---

44   CAA airport statistics 2011 and DfT analysis of CAA airport statistics 2011
45   The list of airports is available at: http://www.cbp.gov/xp/cgov/toolbox/contacts/preclear_locations.xml
46   http://www.cbp.gov/xp/cgov/travel/trusted_traveler/
47   http://www.ukba.homeoffice.gov.uk/customs-travel/Enteringtheuk/usingiris/

we are to prevent illegal immigration, turn away criminals and maintain Britain's secure borders.

1.73   Whilst the safety and security of the public is our priority, we accept that we have a responsibility to process genuine, low-risk passengers without delay. We fully recognise the importance of a positive first experience at the border and that long queues to enter our country make a bad first impression. The UK border experience during the London 2012 Olympic and Paralympic Games was first class and we aim to maintain a high standard for the future. This is why the Government has already started the recruitment of around 600 extra Border Force staff, of which 425 are for Heathrow airport, to provide additional flexibility to secure the border while dealing with increased passenger numbers.

Supporting passengers during disruption at airports

1.74   The above measures aim to reduce disruption for passengers. However, when disruption does occur or when it is very likely to occur, good planning within the airport community and good communication with passengers can minimise a poor passenger experience. In addition, airlines have obligations under European law to ensure passenger welfare, and the CAA is working to achieve routine compliance with passenger rights.

Encouraging new routes and services

Liberalisation of air services

1.75   The opening up of air services to genuine competition has driven down the cost of air transport and greatly improved the range and quality of services. We will continue to seek to liberalise the bilateral air services agreements that govern flights beyond the EU to enable airlines to provide services freely on the basis of commercial considerations. For example, we have recently modernised our agreements with key emerging markets, including China, Vietnam and Indonesia. We are also seeking to modernise our agreements with a range of other countries, including Russia and Egypt, to meet increasing demand.

1.76   Building on the success of the Olympics and the GREAT brand marketing we are working hard to set out the UK's international air services policy and what we are doing to support new international routes and services, airports in Northern Ireland, Scotland and Wales and regional airports in England. These new services will benefit businesses and passengers alike, supporting jobs and growth.

1.77   We will also continue to work closely with the European Commission and other Member States in seeking to develop liberalised EU-level air transport agreements with other countries and to seek the relaxation of restrictions on cross-border investment in order to allow UK airlines greater access to foreign capital and to allow them greater freedom to invest in foreign airlines.

Extending fifth freedoms to Gatwick, Stansted and Luton

1.78 Fifth freedoms are the rights granted to allow an airline of one country to land in a different country, pick up passengers and carry them on to a third country. The UK has long had a general presumption in favour of liberalising fifth freedoms from airports outside the South East.

1.79 To improve connectivity at an international level and to help make better use of existing infrastructure at London's congested airports, we announced in 2011 that we would consult on extending the UK's existing regional fifth freedoms policy to Gatwick, Stansted and Luton.[48] The granting of fifth freedoms would allow a foreign airline to carry passengers between these three London airports and another country as part of a service that begins or ends in the airline's home country. For example, a Singaporean airline would be able to operate a service from Changi Airport in Singapore to Gatwick Airport and then on to JFK Airport in the US, picking up passengers at Gatwick Airport and carrying them to New York.

1.80 The CAA found that in the case of airports outside the South East such a policy would deliver net benefits to UK interests. The Government believes that extending the policy to include Gatwick, Stansted and Luton would also benefit the UK, supporting London's and the UK's aviation connectivity and attracting new services and additional stop-over flights to these airports.

1.81 This policy would be subject to the same conditions that apply to the UK's existing regional fifth freedoms policy,[49] namely that the grant of such rights would be subject to a case-by-case consideration within the context of the current position in the UK's bilateral aviation relationship with the country concerned (for example, we might not grant such rights if there were concerns that there was not a level competitive playing field in the market, such as if it were argued that the airline in question was in receipt of state aid that was distorting competition, or if the grant of such rights was felt likely to significantly diminish the possibility of securing a wider liberalisation that would deliver additional consumer benefits or if it was felt likely to result in significant and sustained disbenefits to consumers by restricting choice and value on a specific route).

Airport slots

1.82 We consider it important that an effective slot allocation regime continues to operate at the UK's airports. We continue to support the core principle of the European Union's Airport Slot Regulation, which is that airlines should have fair and equal access to airports across the EU through independent and transparent slot allocation procedures.

---

48 *National Infrastructure Plan*, HM Treasury-Infrastructure UK, November 2011,
    http://cdn.hm-treasury.gov.uk/national_infrastructure_plan291111.pdf
49 *Relaxation of restrictions on international services from UK regional airports*, DfT, June 2011,
    http://www.dft.gov.uk/publications/relaxation-of-restrictions-on-international-services-from-uk-regional-airports

1.83   We also support the central objective of proposed revisions to the existing Slot Regulation set out within the European Commission's *Better Airports Package*.[50] This aims to promote the most effective use of airport slots and build on the existing transparent, commercial market-based approach to encourage more efficient use of limited capacity, reduce delays, and thereby improve the experience for passengers at congested airports.

1.84   We are committed to engaging constructively at European-level discussions with the aim of supporting proposals that have been demonstrated to improve slot utilisation. Discussions remain ongoing. We continue to work closely with the European Commission to assess carefully any proposals and their potential impacts on the UK aviation industry's commercial interests.

1.85   To ensure the most economically beneficial use of slots at our congested airports, we are working within the EU legislative framework to optimise the commercial market for the trading of airport slots by airlines in the UK (known as secondary trading).

Maintaining a viable network of business and general aviation

1.86   Across the UK there is a network of aerodromes of varying sizes, from airports in Northern Ireland, Scotland, Wales and regional airports in England to small business and general aviation (GA) airfields into which GA aircraft can readily gain access. While almost all of these are privately owned and operated, maintaining access to such a national network is vital to the continuing success of the sector.

1.87   Business and general aviation connects many UK and international destinations that do not have, and are unlikely to develop, scheduled air services or other direct transport links. GA aerodromes can also complement commercial air transport and provide increased connectivity at important hubs such as London. These links are particularly important for local businesses. Ninety-six per cent of city pairs served by business aviation have no scheduled connection.[51]

1.88   Given the importance of this GA network, while recognising that in congested airports this may not be appropriate, we encourage airport operators to ensure that GA aircraft are able to continue to enjoy equitable access to their airports and in doing so take account of the needs of all users, alongside other relevant considerations.

1.89   We will also carefully consider any EU legislative proposals affecting the GA sector that may emerge in the future and will seek to ensure that they are based on the principles of proportionality and subsidiarity and appropriate for the type of aircraft to which they apply. In addition, we support the

50   The European Commission's *Better Airports Package* was launched in December 2011, http://ec.europa.eu/transport/air/airports/airports_en.htm

51   *The Role of Business Aviation in the European Economy*, Oxford Economics, October 2012

CAA's review of the regulatory approach to recreational aviation,[52] which is also aimed at ensuring that UK safety regulation is proportionate.

1.90 The planning system also has a bearing on the operation of small and medium-sized aerodromes. The *National Planning Policy Framework* (NPPF)[53] is intended to simplify the Government's overarching planning policy, but the underlying planning principles in respect of airfields remain unaltered. The NPPF states "when planning for ports, airports and airfields that are not subject to a separate national policy statement, plans should take account of their growth and role in serving business, leisure, training and emergency service need. Plans should take account of this framework as well as the principles set out in the relevant national policy statements and the Government Framework for UK Aviation".

1.91 Where a planning application is made that is likely to have an impact on an existing aerodrome's operations, the economic benefit of the aerodrome and its value to the overall aerodrome network as well the economic benefits of the development will be considered as part of the application process. However, these benefits will be balanced against all other considerations. This is also something which could be considered by airport consultative committees (ACCs) where appropriate (see Chapter 4).

Integrating airports in the wider transport network (short term)

Rail access to airports

1.92 Significant investments are already being made or committed, for example Gatwick Airport's station and improving Thameslink services to Gatwick and Luton. A new fleet of electric trains has been introduced on the Stansted Express. Access to Manchester Airport is being improved through the measures set out in Chapter 5, as well as through delivery of electrification programmes in the North of England and the elements of the Northern Hub[54] which have already been announced.

1.93 Rail offers opportunities for efficient and environmentally-friendly connections to airports, particularly for larger airports where passenger numbers are sufficient to justify fast and frequent services. We will continue our work with airport operators, the rail industry, local authorities and Local Enterprise Partnerships (LEPs) to improve rail access to our airports in the coming years.

1.94 For example, we are providing funding for a new rail line between the Great Western Main Line and Heathrow which could provide significantly improved connections from the Thames Valley, the West of England and Wales to the airport and journey time savings of up to 30 minutes.

---

52 *Strategic Review of General Aviation in the UK*, CAA, July 2006, http://www.caa.co.uk/docs/33/StrategicReviewGA.pdf
53 *National Planning Policy Framework*, Department of Communities and Local Government, March 2012,
http://www.communities.gov.uk/documents/planningandbuilding/pdf/2116950.pdf
54 More information on the Northern hub is available here: http://www.northernhub.co.uk/

1.95 The Department for Transport is working with the rail industry, operators of some of our biggest airports and other key stakeholders to identify further opportunities to improve rail surface access and agree how these might be delivered.

Improving surface access to airports

1.96 High quality, efficient and reliable road and rail access to airports contributes greatly to the experience of passengers, freight operators and people working at the airport. Greater use of low carbon modes to access airports also has the potential to reduce CO_2 emissions, as well as leading to less congestion and improved air quality.

1.97 We are committed to working with airport operators, transport operators, local authorities and LEPs to improve surface access to airports across the country, whilst taking into account the associated environmental impacts. We are already contributing funding to make this happen. For example, through the Regional Growth Fund (RGF), the Government has awarded:

- £19.5 million to Luton Borough Council for junction enhancements which will improve access from the M1 to Luton Airport;

- £18 million to Doncaster Borough Council for the *'Gateway to the Sheffield City Region'*. This is an infrastructure project to improve access to the Sheffield area. The RGF grant will be used towards the construction of a link road between Doncaster and Robin Hood Airport.

1.98 On the strategic road network, we have committed investment for major enhancement projects that will improve airport access, such as the £150 million scheme to widen the A453 near Nottingham where construction started in January 2013. This improvement will widen the route between the M1 and East Midlands Airport, facilitating access for both passengers and air freight operators. We have also announced development of future major proposals to increase capacity on the M4 between junctions 3 and 12, which will improve journeys towards Heathrow Airport.

Strategy for a vibrant aviation sector: the medium and long term

Integrating airports in the wider transport network (medium and long term)

1.99 Through its Long Term Planning Process, Network Rail, in conjunction with airport and train operators, local authorities and LEPs is considering options for enhancing rail services to major airports. Route-based studies will assess the case for taking forward options relating to individual airports alongside the future needs of rail passengers and freight customers as a whole. Where a good case for train service improvements to airports is identified, the DfT will consider them for potential delivery through its High

Level Output Specification for the railway and through its franchising activities.

Developing a national high rail network

1.100 The Government will ensure that its national strategies for aviation and high-speed rail are aligned, providing a better travel offer to the UK travelling public

1.101 International experience shows that rail can be an attractive and convenient form of travel for inter-urban journeys, enabling people to travel directly from city centre to city centre. An important part of our approach is to enable more people to take the train, instead of air transport, for domestic and short-haul European journeys, both in order to achieve environmental benefits and to release capacity at airports. However, we recognise that there will always be a need for domestic aviation; for example, for connections to Northern Ireland and the Scottish islands and other parts of the UK not served by rail, for cross-country routes, and for express freight onward journeys.

1.102 The full 'Y' network will enable fully high-speed services to Manchester, the East Midlands, South Yorkshire and Leeds, and the operation of 'classic compatible' trains on the network will further reduce journey times to Scotland and the North West, as well as enabling high-speed services to reach new destinations in Yorkshire and the North East via the East Coast Main Line. These links will bring Glasgow and Edinburgh within 3 hours and 40 minutes of central London by rail, a journey time comparable with aviation, and reduce the rail journey time from London to Newcastle to just over 2 hours. We estimate that, with the Y network in place, as many as 5.4 million trips a year could be made by rail which might otherwise have been made by air.

1.103 From 2026, when Phase One opens, rail passengers into Heathrow would start to benefit from significantly faster journey times. This would mark a major improvement in rail access to Heathrow compared with today. Passengers from the Midlands and North would be able to access the Heathrow Express service from Old Oak Common station, which would provide an 11-minute connection into the airport. Rail journeys from the Midlands and the North would be as much as 50% quicker, involving fewer changes, and it would no longer be necessary to travel via central London.

1.104 The Government also supports a direct high-speed connection to Heathrow, as there is a case for providing significant rail capacity to the country's major hub airport. Following a public consultation in 2011, the Government concluded that it was important that High Speed 2 (HS2) should serve Heathrow directly; that the optimal approach would be via a spur off the main HS2 line and that this should be built as part of Phase Two of the HS2 network, opening in 2032/33.

1.105 The Government continues to support the principle of integrating HS2 with our country's airports. We consider, however, that further work on a link to Heathrow should now await the consideration of the conclusions and recommendations of the Airports Commission. We will therefore pause work on the Heathrow spur until the Commission's recommendations have been considered.

1.106 In view of this pause in work, the proposals for the Heathrow spur and station are not planned to be part of the Phase Two consultation. However, there would still be the opportunity to consult separately at a later point and include the Heathrow spur in legislation for Phase Two without any impact on the delivery time if that fits with the recommendations of the Commission.

1.107 To avoid severe disruption to the Phase One line after it has opened, however, the Government would consider carrying out the preparatory construction work needed to preserve the option of our preference for serving Heathrow in the future. Including this work now could save significant disruption and cost at a later point.

1.108 The Government following the next General Election will decide on the best way to serve Heathrow by HS2.

Conclusions

1.109 We have set out above a strategy based on practical measures which we believe will improve the use of existing runways across the UK and ease pressure on our hub airport in the short term and into the medium and long term with the development of HS2. However, beyond 2020, we recognise that even with HS2 in place, using current operating techniques, there will be a capacity challenge at the biggest airports in the South East of England. The five London airports were at 78% capacity in 2010 and they are forecast to be 91% full in 2020 and totally full by around 2030. Heathrow is in practice already operating at maximum air transport movement (ATM) capacity.

1.110 Our long-term objective remains **to ensure that the UK's air links continue to make it one of the best connected countries in the world. This includes increasing our links to emerging markets so that the UK can compete successfully for economic growth opportunities**.

1.111 We isrecognise that this raises difficult issues and the need for serious answers to tough questions. For this reason, as previously mentioned, we have established the independent Airports Commission to investigate how to achieve the Government's long-term objectives.

2. Climate change impacts

Context

2.1   Globally, the aviation sector is responsible for about 1 to 2% of greenhouse gas emissions.[55] In the UK, domestic and international aviation[56] emissions account for about 6% of total greenhouse gas emissions or 22% of the transport sector's greenhouse gas emissions. This compares to 40% of the transport sector's greenhouse gas emissions that are emitted by cars, 14% by heavy goods vehicles and 8% by domestic and international shipping.[57] Aviation is, however, likely to make up an increasing proportion of the UK's total greenhouse gas emissions, while other sectors decarbonise more quickly over time.

2.2   Aviation's most significant contribution to climate change in the longer term is through emissions of carbon dioxide (CO_2), which make up about 99% of the sector's Kyoto basket of greenhouse gas emissions,[58] and this has therefore been the focus of government action. But we recognise that the complexities of atmospheric chemistry mean that the total climate change impacts of aviation are greater than those from its CO_2 emissions alone. Non-CO_2 emissions from aviation can have both cooling and warming effects on the climate, with a likely overall warming impact on the atmosphere. Nitrogen oxides (NO_x), sulphur oxides (SO_x) and water vapour all contribute to the overall effect, with NO_x emissions resulting in the production of ozone, a greenhouse gas and air pollutant with harmful health and ecosystem effects. However, despite advances over the past decade, considerable scientific uncertainty remains about the scale of the effect on climate change of non-CO_2 emissions. As a consequence there is no consensus on whether and how to mitigate them.

---

55   Reducing Transport Greenhouse Gas Emissions: Trends & Data, International Transport Forum, 2010, http://www.internationaltransportforum.org/Pub/pdf/10GHGTrends.pdf Greenhouse Gas Emissions from Aviation and Marine Transportation: Mitigation Potential and Policies, Prepared for the Pew Center on Global Climate Change by David McCollum, Gregory Gould and David Greene, 2009, http://www.c2es.org/docUploads/aviation-and-marine-report-2009.pdf

56   There is currently no internationally agreed way of allocating international emissions to individual countries. The percentage shares are based on the percentage of bunker fuel sales to the aviation sector from the UK.

57   Domestic and international aviation emissions on the basis of bunker fuel sales in the UK to the aviation sector. *UK Greenhouse Gas Emissions*, Department of Energy and Climate Change, 2011, available through https://www.gov.uk/government/publications/final-uk-emissions-estimates

58   Ibid.

2.3   Our focus will remain on actions to target CO_2 emissions, which may also help to reduce some of the non-CO_2 emissions. We will continue to support efforts to improve the understanding of the non-CO_2 impacts of aviation. The UK is participating in and helping to fund a number of projects investigating non-CO_2 impacts such as the effects of contrails and NO_x on atmospheric warming. As scientific understanding improves and evidence of the effects of non-CO_2 emissions becomes clearer, we will adapt our approach as necessary to ensure our strategy addresses aviation's total climate change impacts effectively.

Our climate change strategy for aviation

2.4   **The Government's objective is to ensure that the aviation sector makes a significant and cost-effective contribution towards reducing global emissions.**

2.5   Our emphasis is on action at a global level as the best means of securing our objective, with action within Europe the next best option and a potential step towards wider international agreement. We will also take unilateral action at a national level where that is appropriate and justified in terms of the balance between benefits and costs. This is, however, more difficult to achieve for international flights due to the risks of market distortions.

Policy measures: action at a global level

2.6   Flights departing from UK airports to international destinations account for about 95% of UK aviation emissions,[59] so measures to tackle CO_2 emissions would benefit from an international approach determined through bilateral or multilateral agreements. Greenhouse gases emitted anywhere in the world contribute to a global problem, which is why we believe we require a globally agreed solution.

2.7   The UK has played a leading role in securing progress internationally, both within the International Civil Aviation Organization (ICAO) and within the EU. The global nature of the climate change challenge and the international character of the aviation industry make a strong case for a global deal on emissions that is comprehensive, non-discriminatory and ensures that CO_2 emissions are not simply displaced elsewhere. The greatest contribution that any single state can make to reducing aviation emissions is to actively support steps towards such a global deal. The UK will therefore continue to push for an international agreement to ensure that action is taken at the right level and do everything we can to bring others along with us.

2.8   Action at a global level is the preferred and most effective means by which to reduce emissions. Taking action only at a national or regional level has the potential to create the risk of carbon leakage with passengers travelling via other countries and increasing emissions elsewhere. In other words, if

---

59   Measured on a bunker fuel sales basis. *Transport Statistics Great Britain,* DfT, 2011, http://www.dft.gov.uk/statistics/releases/transport-statistics-great-britain-2011.

action at the national or regional level increases the price of air fares only on certain routes, it is possible that some passengers could choose to travel on alternative routes which are outside the scope of such action.

The international aviation industry

2.9 The international aviation industry has also made progress in developing an agreed strategy to reduce its emissions. Airlines, represented by the International Air Transport Association (IATA), have set targets for a 1.5% average annual improvement in fuel efficiency to 2020, to deliver carbon-neutral growth through a cap on 'net' emissions (taking account of emissions trading) from 2020 onwards and to cut net emissions in half by 2050 compared with 2005 levels.[60]

The International Civil Aviation Organization (ICAO)

2.10 The Government will continue to support action through ICAO towards a global agreement to address the climate change emissions from aviation. While we would have preferred to see more rapid progress, steps are being made in the right direction.

2.11 The Government recognises the significant potential for global action in this area, and fully supports the work being undertaken by ICAO this year to work towards developing a global market-based measure to tackle CO_2 emissions from international aviation and a framework for market-based measures.

2.12 The Government recognises the significant potential for global action in this area, and fully supports the work being undertaken by ICAO this year to provide guidance on the development of a framework for market-based measures and the evaluation of the feasibility of options for a global market-based measure to tackle greenhouse gas emissions from international aviation and on the other key areas in the field of international aviation and climate change. This includes sustainable alternative fuels for aviation, global aspirational goals, States' action plans, and assistance to States.

2.13 In addition to assessing the feasibility of market-based measures, ICAO has also committed, through its Committee on Aviation Environmental Protection (CAEP), to agreeing an international CO_2 standard for aircraft by 2016 which aims to reward and encourage improvements in technology to reduce emissions.

2.14 ICAO has also agreed a global aspirational goal of carbon neutral growth from 2020, and through the use of technology, operations, alternative fuels and economic instruments, has agreed a goal of annual fuel efficiency improvements of 2% per year globally out to 2050 – slightly higher than the industry goal.[61] We fully support these developments and will continue to press for more progress to be made.

---

60 IATA, A global approach to reducing aviation emissions, available at
http://www.iata.org/whatwedo/environment/Documents/global-approach-reducing-missions.pdf

61 See, for example, http://www.icao.int/Newsroom/Pages/icao-environmental-meeting-commits-to-a-co2-standard.aspx

> ### 'Gross' versus 'net' emissions
>
> The level of 'gross' emissions from a particular sector is the actual quantity of emissions emitted by the sector. The 'net' emissions for the sector take account of the emissions allowances or international project credits that it has traded with other sectors. For example, a sector in the EU Emissions Trading System may be given a cap of 80 million tonnes of CO_2 ($MtCO_2$) and allocated allowances to this level. If the sector actually emits 100 MtCO2, it will need to purchase an additional 20 $MtCO_2$ of allowances or credits (representing emissions savings) from other sectors in order for the overall cap to be met. This sector would be said to have gross emissions of 100 $MtCO_2$ and net emissions of 80 $MtCO_2$ (100 $MtCO_2$ gross emissions minus 20 $MtCO_2$ of purchased allowances or credits).

Policy measures: action at a European level

2.15   In the absence of an ambitious legally binding global agreement to tackle aviation emissions, our strategy is to continue to strongly support action at a European level. The EU has agreed a comprehensive strategy to tackle climate change emissions based upon four pillars: reduction of emissions at source; research and development; modernisation of air traffic management and market-based measures. Two of the key components of the strategy are including aviation in the EU Emissions Trading System (EU ETS) from 2012 and improving EU airspace design through the Single European Sky programme.

EU Emissions Trading System (EU ETS)

2.16   UK[62] and international[63] aviation gross emissions are forecast to increase out to 2050 without additional action. However, as part of the EU ETS, flights covered by the scheme are subject to an emissions cap (limit) in 2012 of 97% of average annual emissions between 2004 and 2006. In 2013 this cap was reduced to 95%. This means that net emissions from flights arriving into and departing from European Economic Area (EEA) airports cannot increase above the level of the cap.

2.17   To stay within the EU ETS cap, airlines can either reduce their own emissions over time, or purchase allowances or credits from other sectors where options for reducing CO_2 are easier and cheaper to deliver. As noted in responses to the scoping document, airlines already have a considerable cost incentive to reduce fuel consumption, which directly reduces emissions. By effectively putting a price on CO_2 emissions the EU ETS provides an additional financial incentive to invest in low carbon technologies and more efficient operational practices.

2.18   The Government believes that the EU ETS is a cost-effective means of achieving a specified level of emissions. The overall cap places a limit on the

---

62   DfT, UK Aviation Forecasts 2013, available at https://www.gov.uk/government/publications/uk-aviation-forecasts-2013.
63   See, for example, http://legacy.icao.int/icao/en/env2010/Pubs/EnvReport2010/ICAO_EnvReport10-Outlook_en.pdf

total CO_2 emissions from all of the sectors that are members of the scheme. The ability of sectors with the lowest abatement costs to sell their surplus allowances to those whose abatement costs are higher ensures that emission reductions within the EU ETS are made wherever it is cheapest to do so.

2.19 Reducing emissions from within the aviation sector is anticipated to be more difficult and more costly than in other industries.[64] Therefore, to achieve a given level of emissions savings, it is expected that aircraft operators would purchase allowances or credits from other sectors, at least in the short to medium term.

2.20 The EU ETS has a number of flexibilities that enable changes to be agreed which can increase the environmental ambition. For example, over time the emissions cap could be reduced to ensure consistency with agreed national and international targets. Currently the EU ETS is designed to deliver its share of emissions savings under the EU goal of reducing greenhouse gas emissions by 20% by 2020, which includes international aviation emissions, and under current legislation will continue to reduce emissions at a rate of 1.74% a year. The UK's Impact Assessment in 2010 estimated that aviation's inclusion in the EU ETS will reduce net CO_2 emissions from flights arriving at and departing from EU airports by about 480 million tonnes of CO_2 ($MtCO_2$) between 2012 and 2020, and by around 80 $MtCO_2$ in 2020.[65] Beyond 2020, the EU ETS could be used to deliver longer-term targets consistent with the internationally agreed goal to limit the rise in average global temperature to below 2 degrees Celsius. The aviation emissions cap could therefore be adjusted accordingly to deliver a fair contribution from the sector to such targets.

2.21 In response to some promising signs of progress towards a global deal at the UN International Civil Aviation Organization (ICAO), the European Commission proposed to 'stop the clock' on the implementation of the international aspects of the Aviation ETS in November 2012. If this proposal is agreed by the EU Member States and the European Parliament it would defer the obligation on aircraft operators to surrender emissions allowances for their flights between EU destinations and non-EU destinations for one year. Obligations on aircraft operators which fly within the EU will remain. The European Commission has said that if sufficient progress is made at this year's ICAO General Assembly, it will propose appropriate further legislation action. We are committed to working within ICAO to make progress on a global agreement at this year's ICAO General Assembly.

2.22 The UK welcomes the Commission's initiative to 'stop the clock' in return for progress on a global agreement in ICAO. We will continue to engage

64 A Marginal Abatement Cost Curve Model for the UK Aviation Sector, EMRC and AEA, 2011, http://assets.dft.gov.uk/publications/response-ccc-report/mac-report.pdf (for example)
65 UK Impact Assessment for the Second Stage Transposition of EU Legislation to include Aviation in the European Union Emissions Trading System (EU ETS), DECC, 2010, http://www.legislation.gov.uk/uksi/2010/1996/pdfs/uksiem_20101996_en.pdf

constructively with the Commission on this proposal. We remain committed to ensuring that the EU ETS is a success.

Implementing the Single European Sky (SES programme)

2.23   A safe and efficient airspace both in the UK and overseas is (along with other changes) an essential ingredient in allowing aviation to grow and in ensuring that its environmental effects are mitigated as much as practicable. The SES initiative aims to enhance design, management and regulation of airspace across the EU by moving from airspace divided by national boundaries to the use of 'functional airspace blocks' (FABs), the boundaries of which are designed to maximise the efficiency of airspace.

2.24   The Government remains a strong supporter of the SES initiative, which is already delivering and expected to deliver further significant benefits not only in terms of punctuality and resilience but also in reduced CO_2 emissions and mitigation of local environmental impacts. The UK will maintain its strong support for the successful implementation of the SES across the EU.

2.25   Within the UK, our commitment to SES has been demonstrated by the establishment of the first FAB in the EU, with Ireland in 2008. This is delivering real benefits including CO_2 reduction through greater flight and fuel efficiency. It is estimated that the UK–Ireland FAB has provided approximately £37.5 million of savings from 2008 to 2011, including around 48,000 tonnes of fuel (around 152,000 tonnes of CO_2).[66] In 2011 alone, the total savings were estimated to be £21.1 million, including 24,000 tonnes of fuel valued at the equivalent of £15.3 million. Based on the current work programme, it is estimated that by 2020 annual savings could reach £31.2 million,[67] including 35,000 tonnes of fuel and 111,000 tonnes of CO_2.

2.26   The UK–Ireland FAB is working actively to enhance its links with air navigation service providers in other European countries with a view to further improving efficiency in the future, potentially leading to a FAB covering a wider area. The UK is also working closely with the adjoining FAB Europe Central (FABEC) States and will continue to do so over the coming years.[68]

The CAA's Future Airspace Strategy (FAS)

2.27   The Government is also a keen supporter of the Civil Aviation Authority's (CAA's) Future Airspace Strategy (FAS),[69] which is considering strategic airspace issues for the UK over the medium and long term with the overall aim of modernising the UK's airspace system in the context of SES objectives. The implementation of the FAS can also play a significant role in delivering our economic and environmental objectives in relation to aviation,

---

66   *UK-Ireland FAB annual report 2011*, NATS, 31 May 2012,
      http://www.nats.co.uk/wp-content/uploads/2012/07/UK-Ireland-FAB-Report-2011.pdf
67   All £ figures in this paragraph were converted from Euros at a rate of 1:1.16 (Correct at 26/02/13, www.xe.com)
68   The FABEC States are France, Germany, Belgium, Luxembourg, the Netherlands and Switzerland.
69   Future Airspace Strategy, CAA, June 2011, http://www.caa.co.uk/docs/2065/20110630FAS.pdf

for example by improving our use of existing capacity by enhancing queue management techniques at busy airports. This provides opportunities to improve fuel efficiency by reducing the amount of airborne holding. The total benefits of FAS are estimated to be in the range of £1.88–£2.45 billion (net present value, 2011 prices) from 2013 to 2030.[70]

2.28   The CAA is leading the overall FAS project but the onus is on the aviation industry to implement it. In December 2012, the Future Airspace Strategy Industry Implementation Group presented its plan to implement the strategy. The Government urges the industry to do what it can to push the plan forward as soon as possible. However, any proposed changes to airspace routes or operating procedures need to be consulted on, and approved by the CAA, and the well-established process for doing this will continue.

Policy measures: action at a national level

2.29   While the main focus of our strategy is to tackle international aviation emissions at an international level, there are a number of actions we are considering or already taking at a national level to support the effective working of the EU ETS and help reduce international emissions. For example, our intention is to update the guidance the Secretary of State for Transport gives to the CAA on its environmental objectives relating to the exercise of its air navigation functions by the end of 2013.

The Climate Change Act 2008

2.30   The Climate Change Act 2008[71] commits the UK to reducing its net greenhouse gas emissions by at least 80% below the baseline[72] by 2050 ('the target'), and requires the Government to set five-yearly carbon budgets, establishing a path towards meeting that target. Emissions from international aviation (and international shipping) currently do not form part of the target, as defined by the Act. The Act required the Government to set out the circumstances and extent to which emissions from international aviation (and international shipping) would be included in carbon budgets before the end of 2012, or explain to Parliament why it has not done so.

2.31   In December 2012, the Government laid a report before Parliament[73] deferring a decision on whether to include international aviation and shipping emissions in carbon budgets until June 2016, in advance of the setting of the 5th Carbon Budget. This approach will allow international negotiations relating to the aviation EU ETS to be resolved before this decision is taken.

---

70   Future Airspace Strategy Deployment Plan, iteration 3, version 1.2, December 2012
     http://www.caa.co.uk/docs/2408/FAS%20Deployment%20Plan.pdf
71   Climate Change Act 2008, http://www.legislation.gov.uk/ukpga/2008/27/contents
72   The baseline is 1990 levels for carbon dioxide, nitrous oxide and methane, and 1995 levels for hydrofluorocarbons, perfluorocarbons and sulphur hexafluoride
73   'International aviation and shipping emissions and the UK's carbon budgets and 2050 target', www.gov.uk/government/publications/uk-carbon-budgets-and-the-2050-target-international-aviation-and-shipping-emissions

2.32   Existing carbon budgets out to 2027 have already been set to leave headroom for international aviation and shipping emissions, putting the UK on a trajectory which would be consistent with a 2050 target that includes a share of international aviation and international shipping emissions and aligns with the UK's share of the international goal of limiting global temperature rises to below 2 degrees Celsius. The Government does not intend to alter the way in which international aviation and international shipping emissions have been taken into account in carbon budgets 1 to 4.

2050 aviation CO_2 target

2.33   In the context of the previous administration's decision to support a third runway at Heathrow, the last Government announced a target to reduce emissions from UK aviation to below 2005 levels by 2050 (the 2050 aviation CO_2 target). It asked the Committee on Climate Change (CCC) to provide advice on options for reducing CO_2 emissions from UK aviation to achieve this. The CCC published its report in December 2009.[74] This Government subsequently commissioned further analytical work to assess the potential for reducing CO_2 emissions from different policy measures and the relative costs of doing so, the results of which were published in August 2011[75] as part of our response to the CCC report.[76]

2.34   Responses to the Aviation Policy Framework Consultation demonstrated both significant support for and significant opposition to the adoption of a sector-specific national aviation target. Those in favour argued that the Government should use all the mechanisms available and a national target would signal a strong commitment to tackling climate change.

2.35   Those against were concerned that a unilateral target would put the UK aviation industry at a competitive disadvantage in the international market, and damage the UK's connectivity, without reducing overall emissions. This is because any reduction in emissions from aviation would reduce the aviation sector's demand for EU ETS allowances. Potential reductions from other sectors would be replaced with emission reductions from the aviation sector. As the abatement of emissions is generally more expensive in aviation than in other EU ETS sectors, delivering the national aviation target would therefore result in a higher cost to achieve the same level of emission reductions as the EU ETS by itself. Therefore, before making a decision on whether the UK should retain a national emissions target for aviation, the Government believes that it is important to have greater certainty over the future scope of the EU ETS and await the outcome of the ICAO negotiations towards a global deal on aviation emissions.

---

74   *Meeting the UK aviation target – options for reducing emissions to 2050*, Committee on Climate Change, December 2009, http://www.theccc.org.uk/reports/aviation-report

75   A Marginal Abatement Cost Curve Model for the UK Aviation Sector, EMRC and AEA , 2011, http://assets.dft.gov.uk/publications/response-ccc-report/mac-report.pdf

76   *Government response to the Committee on Climate Change report on reducing CO_2 emissions from UK aviation to 2050*, DfT, August 2011, http://www.dft.gov.uk/publications/reducing-co2-emissions

UK aviation industry

2.36 Sustainable Aviation, a UK industry coalition of airlines, airports, aerospace manufacturers and air navigation service providers, has set out a roadmap[77] describing how, in a similar way to the IATA target, net CO_2 emissions from UK aviation can be halved by 2050, through technological improvements and carbon trading, against a 2005 baseline. The Government welcomes these developments as a clear indication that the aviation industry is taking the problem seriously. We urge the industry to strive towards achieving these objectives and, over time, to raise its level of ambition.

2.37 The aerospace manufacturing industry recognises that the predicted level of future growth sharpens the emphasis on environmental concerns. Manufacturers have been responsible for most of the reductions in CO_2, NOx and noise over the past 20 years[78] and they are committed to maintaining this rate of reduction. The sector consistently spends between £100 million and £150 million a year[79] on long-term research and technology for civil aircraft, much of which is targeted at environmental improvement. The total civil research and development expenditure is £970 million, which, when combined with civil sales of £11.78 billion corresponds to 8.2% of sales for R&D. This is a high percentage for any UK sector, and indicates that the industry acknowledges and is working to address the problem.

2.38 The future commitment of the UK and the industry across Europe was set out in the original ACARE (Advisory Council for Aeronautics Research in Europe) Strategic Research Agenda from 2002, which set challenging goals for environmental improvement (50% CO_2 reduction, 80% NOx reduction, and halving perceived noise). These goals were for technology readiness in 2020 based on equipment in service in 2000. Evaluations indicate that about two-thirds of these improvements have been or will be achieved through existing programmes by 2020. These targets have recently been superseded by the Flightpath 2050 Report, which set the industry more challenging goals for 2050, and a new Strategic Research and Innovation Agenda for aviation, produced by a new ACARE (now the Advisory Council for Aviation Research and Innovation in Europe) has just been published.

Taxation

2.39 A number of respondents made reference to environmental taxation measures which could incentivise further emission reductions, such as taxing aviation fuel.

2.40 The UK's international obligations in this area include Air Service Agreements with over 150 different countries and the 1944 Chicago Convention. These rules prohibit the taxation of international aviation fuel.

77 *CO_2 Roadmap*, Sustainable Aviation, February 2012,
    http://www.sustainableaviation.co.uk/wp-content/uploads/SA-CO2-Road-Map-full-report-280212.pdf
78 http://www.theccc.org.uk/publication/meeting-the-uk-aviation-target-options-for-reducing-emissions-to-2050/
79 UK Aerospace Survey 2012, an ADS publication, available at http://www.adsgroup.org.uk/pages/35926020.asp

2.41 The EU VAT Directive also applies a mandatory exemption to international passenger transport, which means that it is not possible to charge VAT on international flights. Furthermore, all domestic passenger transport in the UK is currently charged at a zero rate of VAT. For reasons of fair competition, there are legal barriers to charging VAT on domestic air travel and not other forms of domestic transport.

2.42 Recognising that aviation was otherwise under-taxed, in 1994 the UK Government introduced the air passenger duty (APD), which is fundamentally a revenue-raising tax that meets all our international obligations. Since January 2012, aviation has also been included in the EU Emissions Trading System (EU ETS), as a cost-effective solution to tackling aviation's growing emissions, whilst at the same time enabling long-term sustainable growth in the aviation industry. The Chancellor keeps all taxes under review.

Alternatives to air travel

2.43 Alternatives to travel (ATT), such as the use of teleconferencing, videoconferencing or remote working, could help to reduce the demand for air travel and hence emissions from aviation. While there is some evidence suggesting that meetings based on videoconferencing may be additional, rather than substituting for meetings which require air travel, the success of the World Wildlife Fund's (WWF's) '1-in-5' initiative[80] demonstrates what can be achieved when companies adopt ambitious targets to reduce their air travel. To facilitate this behavioural change, the Government is committed to universal coverage for broadband, investing £530 million to stimulate commercial investment and bring high-speed broadband to rural communities[81] and businesses and £150 million to create 22 'super-connected' cities across the UK, with 80–100 megabits per second broadband and city-wide ultra-fast-speed mobile connectivity. The Department for Transport is also in the process of quantifying the true impacts of ATT on carbon reduction, travel demand management and economic growth.

2.44 The Government is not seeking to dispute the benefits provided by travel between the UK's major towns and cities. We fully accept the economic benefits provided by such journeys. We also accept that there are limits on the impact that improved technologies are likely to have on the demand for travel, not least because a successful video conference may prompt further face-to-face meetings which require travel. Nevertheless, these technologies may offer an appropriate alternative to some types of journey, and they are therefore well worth exploring as part of our strategy for addressing the environmental impact of aviation.

---

80 *Join the One in Five Challenge*, WWF
http://www.wwf.org.uk/how_you_can_help/get_your_business_involved/one_in_five_challenge/
81 'Stimulating private sector investment to achieve a transformation in broadband in the UK by 2015', Department for Culture, Media and Sport, available at
https://www.gov.uk/government/policies/transforming-uk-broadband/supporting-pages/rural-broadband-programme

Developing new technology

2.45 The UK has a strong track record in aviation research, design and manufacturing and is well placed to influence and exploit emerging global markets in low carbon technologies as a whole new generation of aircraft is developed.

2.46 Generally fuel represents around 30% of an airline's operating costs.[82] Pressure from airlines to reduce these costs is driving competition between manufacturers to develop more fuel efficient – and hence more carbon efficient – aircraft, which is good for business, good for consumers and good for the environment.

2.47 Since the 1960s, technological and operational advances have reduced fuel burn, and therefore CO_2 emissions, by 70% per passenger kilometre.[83] In the last ten years, although air traffic has increased by 45%, the demand for jet fuel has increased by only 3%.[84]

2.48 The UK aerospace industry is working on a number of research and technology programmes, including some with support from the UK Government and others with European funding support. These programmes generally involve collaboration between manufacturers and their supply chains. The Government will continue to support and encourage such technological developments through industry-led projects including those listed below:

Research and technology programmes

Key collaborative programmes involving Government support include:

- Airbus-led programmes on Integrated Wing, Next Generation Composite Wing, and Electric Landing Gear, with private and public investment totalling around £140 million;

- Rolls-Royce-led programmes on Environmentally Friendly Engine, Environmental Lightweight Fan and Strategic Investment in Low Carbon Engine Technologies, with investment totalling around £220 million;

- a Goodrich-led programme on Advanced More Electric Systems, with investment totalling around £4 million; and

- an AgustaWestland helicopters-led programme on Rotor Embedded Actuator Control technology, with investments totalling around £9 million.

2.49 The Government also provides tax relief for certain research and development activities. Aerospace manufacturers are collaborating in complementary European programmes through the EC Framework 7

---

82 *Fact Sheet, IATA,* December 2011, http://www.iata.org/pressroom/facts_figures/fact_sheets/Pages/fuel.aspx

83 *Fact sheet,* IATA, December 2011, http://www.iata.org/pressroom/facts_figures/fact_sheets/pages/environment.aspx

84 *Delivering the Future – Global Market Forecast 2011-2030,* Airbus, http://www.airbus.com/company/market/forecast/passenger-aircraft-market-forecast/

Programme and the Clean Sky Joint Technology Initiative, which are providing further access to funding.

2.50   The Department for Business, Innovation and Skills (BIS), in partnership with business, academia and other stakeholders, is working through the Aerospace Growth Partnership (AGP) to identify and develop collaborative research projects, for the technologies that will best position the UK aerospace industry to secure sector growth, including increased levels of high-value work on future aircraft programmes. This research is consistent with technology roadmaps developed through an earlier National Aerospace Technology plan.

Biofuels

2.51   Sustainable biofuels have a role to play in reducing CO_2 emissions from transport, particularly in sectors such as aviation where there are limited alternatives to fossil fuel. It is essential that biofuels lead to a worthwhile reduction in full life-cycle CO_2 emissions, taking into account indirect land use change (ILUC), where production of biofuel from crops grown on existing agricultural land results in the displacement of production on to previously uncultivated land. The aviation sector will be competing with other sectors for limited sources of such sustainable biomass.

2.52   The inclusion of aviation within the EU ETS already provides an incentive to develop sustainable biofuels as an alternative to kerosene, as biofuel-powered flights are given a zero carbon rating under the ETS. The Government needs to provide the right framework to ensure that only sustainable biofuels are used. In 2012 the Government published a co-ordinated, evidence-based bioenergy strategy[85] which looks at the best use of available biomass resources for a long-term transition in technology. The European Commission has now come forward with a proposal designed to address ILUC and negotiations are under way. Given legitimate concerns about the sustainability of some biofuels in relation to ILUC, we have not set increased targets.[86] Once we have a better understanding of these issues we will be in a better position to decide where Government intervention may be justified and the extent to which biofuels offer a way forward.

---

85   *UK Bioenergy Strategy*, Department of Energy and Climate Change, 2012, https://www.gov.uk/government/publications/uk-bioenergy-strategy

86   The UK considers the introduction of 'ILUC factors' applied to feedstock groups, in both the Renewable Energy Directive and the Fuel Quality Directive, to be the most appropriate response to the risk posed by ILUC. This should be accompanied by exemptions for biofuels that can demonstrate that they were produced in a way to have 'low ILUC risk'. 'ILUC factors' is the commonly used name for the approach whereby an estimate of ILUC emissions from biofuel use is included in the calculation of greenhouse gas savings.

Case Study: British Airways–Solena Greensky Low Carbon Fuels Project

British Airways is working with the US-based clean-tech company Solena Fuels to develop Europe's first waste-to-biojet fuel plant, the 'Greensky' project. This first-of-a-kind facility, currently at the planning stage, will be constructed east of London.

The project will use high-temperature gasification to convert 500,000 tonnes of low-value residual waste (i.e. material that is presently going to landfill) into a renewable biosynthetic gas (or 'BioSynGas'). The BioSynGas will then be cleaned and passed through a Fischer-Tropsch unit to produce a biocrude fuel to be upgraded into low carbon fuels yielding 50,000 tonnes each of biojet and biodiesel and 20,000 tonnes of bionaphtha. The process will produce the electricity required to power the plant, leaving approximately 11 MW net of green renewable power to be exported to the grid.

Independent greenhouse gas life cycle analysis has confirmed that the process will meet the sustainability standards required by the EU Renewable Energy Directive and the Roundtable on Sustainable Biofuels. The sustainability benefits of this fuel are wide ranging as using waste avoids the indirect land use change impacts associated with many crop-based biofuels. In addition, the fuels produced are very clean burning and provide air quality benefits as they emit very low levels of particulates. The renewable naphtha can be used to make renewable plastics or blended into transport fuels and the process also produces a solid aggregate material that can be used in construction.

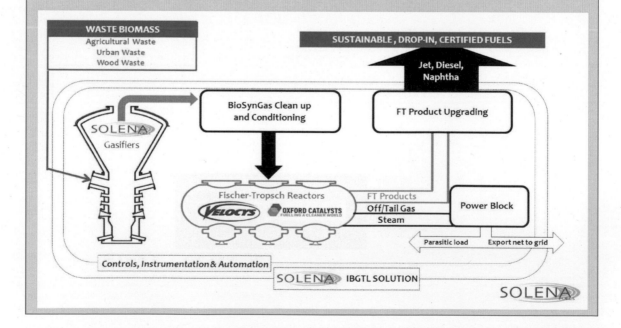

Better information

2.53 Providing consumers with better information to inform their choices can have a powerful effect on corporate behaviour. Many organisations now produce corporate responsibility reports which include the action they are taking to reduce their emissions. Research by Pricewaterhouse Coopers,[87] which looked at reports produced by 46 airlines worldwide, and found some encouraging trends. However, disappointingly, the report also noted that around a third of the airlines studied produced no corporate responsibility reports and that the quality of reporting from those that did was variable.

2.54 The Government strongly supports greater transparency. The Civil Aviation Act, which received Royal Assent on 19 December 2012, contains new information functions for the CAA. These provide scope to increase and improve the quality of information available to the public, including on the environmental effects of civil aviation in the UK and measures taken to limit them, so that environmental performance in relation to CO_2 emissions can become a factor informing consumer decisions. The new information functions for the CAA are discussed further at paragraph 4.9.

Adapting to future climate change

2.55 The Climate Change Act (2008) commits the UK to build resilience to the expected impacts of climate change. It requires the Government to undertake a national Climate Change Risk Assessment (CCRA) every five years and gives Government powers to direct statutory organisations to report on climate change assessments and adaptation actions.[88] In 2013 the Government will publish the first five-year statutory National Adaptation Programme (NAP) setting actions to address climate change challenges.

2.56 Aviation faces many challenges from our changing climate. In 2012 the CAA, NATS and ten airports published climate change adaptation reports under the Climate Change Act Reporting Power. This will be repeated every five years, enabling aviation reporting organisations to produce progress reports.

2.57 These reports highlight climate variables that pose risks to the industry, including increases in extreme weather affecting operations; increases in temperature leading to runway damage; increased rainfall posing flood risk and changes in wind patterns affecting air traffic movements.

2.58 Evidence from these reports and the first CCRA (2012) shows the aviation industry is already taking action to address challenges by, for example, embedding the consideration of climate change in business planning and risk management. Further research is needed to investigate climate

---

87 *'Building trust in the air: Is airline corporate sustainability reporting taking off?'*, PWC, November 2011, http://www.pwc.com/en_GX/gx/sustainability/assets/pwc-airlines-cr.pdf
88 http://www.defra.gov.uk/environment/climate/sectors/reporting-authorities/reporting-authorities-reports/

scenarios, probability of risks, timescales, adaptation options, investments and stakeholder interdependencies.

2.59   The aviation industry will use the NAP to work with Government and other stakeholders in addressing climate risks. The programme will establish a framework in which interdependencies with other sectors can be addressed building cross-cutting resilience.

2.60   The Government strongly supports the need to better understand and manage the risks associated with climate change. It is essential for the successful long-term resilience of the UK's aviation industry and its contribution to supporting economic growth and competitiveness.

3. Noise and other local environmental impacts

Context

3.1   Whilst the aviation industry brings significant benefits to the UK economy, there are costs associated with its local environmental impacts which are borne by those living around airports, some of whom may not use the airport or directly benefit from its operations. This chapter considers noise, air quality and other local environmental impacts.

Noise

3.2   The Government recognises that noise is the primary concern of local communities near airports. The extent to which noise is a source of tension between airports and local communities will vary depending on factors such as the location of an airport in relation to centres of population and the quality of its relations and communications with its local communities. We are aware that many airports already make considerable efforts to engage their local communities and that the relationship is well managed.

3.3   We want to strike a fair balance between the negative impacts of noise (on health, amenity (quality of life) and productivity) and the positive economic impacts of flights. As a general principle, the Government therefore expects that future growth in aviation should ensure that benefits are shared between the aviation industry and local communities. This means that the industry must continue to reduce and mitigate noise as airport capacity grows. As noise levels fall with technology improvements the aviation industry should be expected to share the benefits from these improvements.

3.4   Since England has one of the highest population densities in the EU, it is inevitable that aircraft noise will be a particular issue here compared with other countries. The Government therefore expects the UK aviation industry at all levels (manufacturers, airlines, airports and air traffic service providers) to lead the way in best practice and to drive forward international standards. The Government will also support this effort.

3.5   The Government recognises the good progress already made. We welcome the Noise Roadmap being developed by Sustainable Aviation, which will set out the UK aviation industry's blueprint for managing noise from aviation sources to 2050. Aircraft technology and manufacturing is a UK success story and is driving improvements in the noise performance of new aircraft. The Airbus A380, partially designed and built in the UK, has recently won an award from the Noise Abatement Society for its innovations in quiet technology. The UK was instrumental in securing a recent agreement on a tougher international noise standard in the ICAO Committee on Aviation Environmental Protection (CAEP). This requires new types of large civil aircraft, from 2017, to be at least 7dB quieter in total, across the three test points, than the current standard[89]. Standards for smaller aircraft will be similarly reduced in 2020.

3.6   Our policy on aviation noise will be consistent with agreed international approaches and we will comply with relevant European laws.[90]

3.7   The Government fully recognises the ICAO Assembly 'balanced approach' principle to aircraft noise management.[91] The 'balanced approach' consists of identifying the noise problem at an airport and then assessing the cost-effectiveness of the various measures available to reduce noise through the exploration of four principal elements, which are:

- reduction at source (quieter aircraft);

- land-use planning and management;

- noise abatement operational procedures (optimising how aircraft are flown and the routes they follow to limit the noise impacts); and

- operating restrictions (preventing certain (noisier) types of aircraft from flying either at all or at certain times).

3.8   The International Civil Aviation Organization (ICAO) encourages states not to apply operating restrictions as a first resort but only after consideration of the benefits to be gained from other elements of the balanced approach.

Role of government

The regulated airports

3.9   As well as setting the overall national policy framework for aviation noise, the Government has powers under the Civil Aviation Act 1982 to set noise controls at specific airports which it designates for noise management purposes. When using these powers, our approach will be consistent with

---

89   Based on Effective Perceived Noise Decibels, a specialist noise unit used for aircraft noise certification.
90   Currently these include Directive 2002/30 on the establishment of rules and procedures with regard to the introduction of noise-related operating restrictions at Community airports; Directive 1999/28 amending the Annex to Council Directive 92/14/EEC on the limitation of the operation of aeroplanes covered by Part II, Chapter 2, Volume 1 of Annex 16 to the Convention on International Civil Aviation, second edition (1988); and Directive 2002/49 relating to the assessment and management of environmental noise (the Environmental Noise Directive).
91   Given effect in EU law through Directive 2002/30.

the Government's overall approach to regulation as described in the Executive summary.

3.10 For many years, Heathrow, Gatwick and Stansted Airports have been designated for these purposes, and we will continue to maintain their status. These airports remain strategically important to the UK economy and we therefore consider that it is appropriate for the Government to take decisions on the right balance between noise controls and economic benefits, reconciling the local and national strategic interests. The future of these airports is also under consideration as part of the work of the Airports Commission and it would not be appropriate to change their regulatory status at this time.

3.11 Other airports not currently designated for noise management purposes have powers to set noise controls (see Annex A) and the Government would like appropriate controls to be agreed locally. For example, local authorities will want to consider whether to set such controls as a planning condition on new airport development. Noise controls at the designated airports will provide examples for other airports to consider as appropriate. Airports should ensure that the effectiveness of their measures to tackle noise is reviewed on a regular basis. For airports required to produce Noise Action Plans under EU legislation,[92] this should be done at least as often as the five-yearly review of these plans. Noise Action Plans and any other noise measures agreed locally should be proportionate to actual noise impacts.

Policy objective

3.12 The Government's overall policy on aviation noise is **to limit and, where possible, reduce the number of people in the UK significantly affected by aircraft noise**, as part of a policy of sharing benefits of noise reduction with industry.

3.13 This is consistent with the Government's Noise Policy, as set out in the Noise Policy Statement for England (NPSE)[93] which aims to avoid significant adverse impacts on health and quality of life.

3.14 Although there is some evidence that people's sensitivity to aircraft noise appears to have increased in recent years, there are still large uncertainties around the precise change in relationship between annoyance and the exposure to aircraft noise. There is evidence that there are people who consider themselves annoyed by aircraft noise who live some distance from an airport in locations where aircraft are at relatively high altitudes. Conversely, some people living closer to an airport seem to be tolerant of such noise.

3.15 To provide historic continuity, the Government will continue to ensure that noise exposure maps are produced for the noise-designated airports on an

---

92   The Environmental Noise Directive 2002/49.

93   Noise Policy Statement for England, Defra, March 2010. Comparable principles apply for other parts of the UK.

annual basis providing results down to a level of 57dB LAeq 16 hour.[94] To improve monitoring of the specific impact of night noise, we will also ensure that separate night noise contours for the eight-hour night period (11pm–7am) are produced for the designated airports.

3.16 This does not preclude airports from producing results to a lower level or using other indicators to describe the noise impact of their operations, as appropriate (see paragraph 3.19 below). Some airports already map noise exposure to lower levels every five years under European legislation and we encourage those that routinely produce such contours on a voluntary basis to continue to do so, as a means of facilitating improved monitoring, transparency and communication of the impact of aircraft noise. Other airports which have significant night operations may also wish to produce separate night noise contours on a regular basis.

3.17 We will continue to treat the 57dB LAeq 16 hour contour as the average level of daytime aircraft noise marking the approximate onset of significant community annoyance. However, this does not mean that all people within this contour will experience significant adverse effects from aircraft noise. Nor does it mean that no-one outside of this contour will consider themselves annoyed by aircraft noise.

3.18 The Airports Commission has also recognised that there is no firm consensus on the way to measure the noise impacts of aviation and has stated that this is an issue on which it will carry out further detailed work and public engagement.[95] We will keep our policy under review in the light of any new emerging evidence.

3.19 Average noise exposure contours are a well established measure of annoyance and are important to show historic trends in total noise around airports. However, the Government recognises that people do not experience noise in an averaged manner and that the value of the LAeq indicator does not necessarily reflect all aspects of the perception of aircraft noise. For this reason we recommend that average noise contours should not be the only measure used when airports seek to explain how locations under flight paths are affected by aircraft noise. Instead the Government encourages airport operators to use alternative measures which better reflect how aircraft noise is experienced in different localities,[96] developing these measures in consultation with their consultative committee and local communities. The objective should be to ensure a better understanding of noise impacts and to inform the development of targeted noise mitigation measures.

---

94 The A-weighted average sound level over the 16 hour period of 0700-2300. This is based on an average summer day when producing noise contour maps at the designated airports.

95 Guidance Document 01: Submitting evidence and proposals to the Airports Commission, February 2013.

96 Examples include frequency and pattern of movements and highest noise levels which can be expected.

Land-use planning and management

3.20 Chapter 5 explains the status of the Aviation Policy Framework and its interaction with existing planning guidance and policies. Land-use planning and management is one of the elements of the ICAO balanced approach which should be explored when tackling noise problems at an airport. In line with the Government's noise policy, the Government's National Planning Policy Framework (NPPF) says that planning policies and decisions should aim to avoid a situation where noise gives rise to significant adverse impacts on health and quality of life as a result of new development, and to mitigate and reduce to a minimum other adverse impacts on health and quality of life arising from noise from new development, including through the use of conditions.

3.21 The NPPF expects local planning policies and decisions to ensure that new development is appropriate for its location and the effects of pollution – including noise – on health, the natural environment or general amenity are taken into account. This does not rule out noise-sensitive development in locations that experience aircraft noise. In the same way that some people consider themselves annoyed by aircraft noise even though they live some distance from an airport in locations where aircraft are at relatively high altitudes, other people living closer to an airport seem to be tolerant of aircraft noise and may choose to live closer to the airport to be near to employment or to benefit from the travel opportunities.

3.22 There can also be other good economic or social reasons for noise-sensitive developments to be located in such areas. However, reflecting Government noise policy, the NPPF is quite clear that the planning system should prevent new development being put at unacceptable risk from, or being adversely affected by, unacceptable levels of noise pollution. Local planning authorities therefore have a responsibility to ensure that the land use element of the balanced approach is implemented in the context of their local plan policies, including any on noise. People considering moving to an area which may be affected by existing aircraft noise also have a responsibility to inform themselves of the likely impacts before moving to the area, and airport operators should ensure that all necessary information to inform such decisions is easily accessible.

3.23 Results from the 2011 Census show a general increase in population density. Consequently, within some noise contours around airports, the number of people has increased regardless of any change in noise. The Government will therefore take into account the trends in populations within the contours when monitoring the effectiveness of its overall policy on aviation noise.

Measures to reduce and mitigate noise – the role of industry

3.24 The acceptability of any growth in aviation depends to a large extent on the industry tackling its noise impact. The Government accepts, however, that it is neither reasonable nor realistic for such actions to impose unlimited costs on industry. Instead, efforts should be proportionate to the extent of the noise problem and numbers of people affected.

3.25 As a general principle, the Government expects that at the local level, individual airports working with the appropriate air traffic service providers should give particular weight to the management and mitigation of noise, as opposed to other environmental impacts, in the immediate vicinity of airports, where this does not conflict with the Government's obligations to meet mandatory EU air quality targets. Any negative impacts that this might have on CO_2 emissions should be tackled as part of the UK's overall strategy to reduce aviation emissions, such as the EU Emissions Trading System (ETS). Further guidance on this principle will be published when the Department for Transport updates its guidance to the Civil Aviation Authority (CAA) on environmental objectives relating to the exercise of its air navigation functions (see Chapter 5).

3.26 The Government wishes airports to consider using the powers available to them (see Annex A) to set suitable noise controls such as departure noise limits, minimum height requirements, noise-preferential routes and adherence to continuous descent approach, and where appropriate to enforce these with dissuasive and proportionate penalties. Both the controls and the levels of penalties should be reviewed regularly (at least as often as the Noise Action Plan where applicable) in consultation with local communities and consultative committees, to ensure they remain effective. For the noise-designated airports, the Department's Aircraft Noise Management Advisory Committee will review the departure and arrivals noise abatement procedures, including noise limits and use of penalties, to ensure that these remain appropriately balanced and effective.

3.27 As part of the range of options available for reducing noise, airports should consider using differential landing charges to incentivise quieter aircraft. The Government has asked the CAA to investigate the use of these charges and the CAA will be publishing its findings later this year.

3.28 The Government expects airports to make particular efforts to mitigate noise where changes are planned which will adversely impact the noise environment. This would be particularly relevant in the case of proposals for new airport capacity, changes to operational procedures or where an increase in movements is expected which will have a noticeable impact on local communities. In these cases, it would be appropriate to consider new and innovative approaches such as noise envelopes or provision of respite for communities already affected.

Noise envelopes

3.29 The Government wishes to pursue the concept of noise envelopes as a means of giving certainty to local communities about the levels of noise which can be expected in the future and to give developers certainty on how they can use their airports. Following any such recommendations made by the Airports Commission, in the case of any new national hub airport capacity or any other airport development which is a nationally significant infrastructure project, the Government is likely to develop a National Policy Statement (NPS) to set out the national need for such a project. The Government would determine principles for the noise envelope in the NPS having regard to the following:

- The Government's overall noise policy.

- Within the limits set by the envelope, the benefits of future technological improvements should be shared between the airport and its local communities to achieve a balance between growth and noise reduction.

- The objective of incentivising airlines to introduce the quietest suitable aircraft as quickly as is reasonably practicable.

3.30 At other airports, local communities are encouraged to work with airports to develop acceptable solutions which are proportionate to the scale of the noise problem and be involved in discussions about the acceptable limits of noise. The Government believes that the process of designing and consulting on a noise envelope could be a suitable mechanism to achieve this. The CAA will produce further guidance on the use and types of noise envelopes which may be used in the context of any proposals for new airport capacity and the work of the Airports Commission.

Airspace

3.31 The routes used by aircraft and the height at which they fly are two significant factors that affect the noise experienced by people on the ground. Consistent with its overall policy to limit and where possible reduce the number of people adversely affected by aircraft noise, the Government believes that, in most circumstances, it is desirable to concentrate aircraft along the fewest possible number of specified routes in the vicinity of airports and that these routes should avoid densely populated areas as far as possible. This is consistent with the long-standing concept of noise-preferential routes which departing aircraft are required to follow at many airports, including the noise-designated airports. Within the countryside, in common with other relevant authorities, the CAA has legal duties to have regard to the purposes of National Parks and Areas of Outstanding Natural Beauty and must therefore take these into account when assessing airspace changes.

3.32 However, in certain circumstances, such as where there is intensive use of certain routes, and following engagement with local communities, it may be appropriate to explore options for respite which share noise between communities on an equitable basis, provided this does not lead to significant numbers of people newly affected by noise. Whether concentration or respite is the preferred option, those responsible for planning how airspace is used should ensure that predictability is afforded to local communities, to the extent that this is within their control. Further guidance on these airspace matters will be provided when the Department for Transport updates its guidance to the CAA on environmental objectives relating to the exercise of its air navigation functions (see Chapter 5).

Information and communication

3.33   At all airports, the key principle should be that airports act as good neighbours so that local communities have confidence that airport operators take their noise impacts seriously. This requires airports to be open and transparent in their communications. The Government expects airports to help local communities understand these noise impacts and performance against relevant targets or commitments through monitoring, provision of information and communication designed around the specific noise impacts and the needs of the community. We expect airports to select appropriate tools such as noise monitors (fixed and mobile), online information showing aircraft flight paths, heights and noise, track-keeping, performance reports and metrics which describe noise in ways which communities can easily understand. We encourage the CAA to consider how it can use its information functions (see paragraph 4.25) to share good practice in how airports monitor, report and communicate their noise impacts.

Night noise

3.34   The Government recognises that the costs on local communities are higher from aircraft noise during the night, particularly the health costs associated with sleep disturbance. Noise from aircraft at night is therefore widely regarded as the least acceptable aspect of aircraft operations. However, we also recognise the importance to the UK economy of certain types of flights, such as express freight services, which may only be viable if they operate at night. As part of our current consultation on night flying restrictions at the noise-designated airports, we are seeking evidence on the costs and benefits of night flights.

3.35   In recognising these higher costs upon local communities, we expect the aviation industry to make extra efforts to reduce and mitigate noise from night flights through use of best-in-class aircraft, best practice operating procedures, seeking ways to provide respite wherever possible and minimising the demand for night flights where alternatives are available. We commend voluntary approaches such as the curfew at Heathrow which ensures that early morning arrivals do not land before 4.30am.

Noise insulation and compensation

3.36 The Government continues to expect airport operators to offer households exposed to levels of noise of 69 dB LAeq,16h or more, assistance with the costs of moving.

3.37 The Government also expects airport operators to offer acoustic insulation to noise-sensitive buildings, such as schools and hospitals, exposed to levels of noise of 63 dB LAeq,16h or more. Where acoustic insulation cannot provide an appropriate or cost-effective solution, alternative mitigation measures should be offered.

3.38 If no such schemes already exist, airport operators should consider financial assistance towards acoustic insulation for households. Where compensation schemes have been in place for many years and there are few properties still eligible for compensation, airport operators should review their schemes to ensure they remain reasonable and proportionate.

3.39 Where airport operators are considering developments which result in an increase in noise, they should review their compensation schemes to ensure that they offer appropriate compensation to those potentially affected. As a minimum, the Government would expect airport operators to offer financial assistance towards acoustic insulation to residential properties which experience an increase in noise of 3dB or more which leaves them exposed to levels of noise of 63 dB LAeq,16h or more.

3.40 Any potential proposals for new nationally significant airport development projects following any Government decision on future recommendation(s) from the Airports Commission would need to consider tailored compensation schemes where appropriate, which would be subject to separate consultation.

3.41 Airports may wish to use alternative criteria or have additional schemes based on night noise where night flights are an issue. Airport consultative committees should be involved in reviewing schemes and invited to give views on the criteria to be used.

General aviation and helicopters

3.42 The Government recognises that aviation noise is not confined to large commercial airports and that annoyance can also be caused by smaller aerodromes used for business and general aviation (GA) purposes, especially at times of intensive activity. However, it would not be appropriate for the Government to intervene by exercising powers under section 78 of the Civil Aviation Act 1982 to set noise controls at small aerodromes. Industry has developed codes of practice and the CAA has produced guidance. We would encourage the GA sector and the CAA to review their respective best practice and guidance to reflect the policy adopted in this Policy Framework. We would also encourage the sector to monitor compliance with its codes of practice.

3.43 Government has the power to specify an aerodrome under section 5 of the Civil Aviation Act 1982. The effect of specification of a particular aerodrome is to place a duty on the CAA in exercising its aerodrome licensing functions to have regard to the need to minimise as far as reasonably practicable any adverse effects on the environment and any disturbance to the public from (among other things) noise attributable to the use of aircraft at the aerodrome. The Government is against the use of regulatory solutions where alternatives exist and would not expect to exercise this power until all other avenues can reasonably be said to have been exhausted.

3.44 The Government encourages aerodromes to engage with local communities effectively as a matter of good practice. Moreover, the Government would expect local communities to be involved in all such engagement, and would want to see evidence of this happening before exercising its powers under section 5. An assessment of the extent and nature of noise disturbance and a consultation on any proposed measures to address aircraft noise would provide the basis for informed decision-making by the Government and the CAA.

3.45 Noise from helicopters is perceived as a problem in certain areas, such as routes used intensively by helicopters. The Government commends the British Helicopter Association's Code of Conduct for Pilots[97], which is designed to avoid unnecessary noise intrusion, and urges helicopter operators to promote this as widely as possible. Helicopters must meet internationally agreed noise standards prior to the issue of a Certificate of Airworthiness. Helicopters are also subject to Rules of the Air Regulations, which require minimum heights to be maintained. Whilst this is for safety reasons, these Regulations also offer some noise benefits. In recognition of ongoing concerns about disturbance from helicopter traffic in London, we will continue to monitor the impact of helicopter movements in the London area through the data collected by the CAA. We will also seek to ensure, when updating the guidance on environmental objectives, that the CAA considers opportunities to mitigate helicopter noise when dealing with any relevant airspace change proposals.

Air quality and other local environmental impacts

3.46 Whilst noise is the most obvious local environmental impact of airport operations, airports have a significant impact on other aspects of the local environment, some of which, including air quality, may not be visible.

3.47 Emissions from transport, including at airports, contribute to air pollution. EU legislation sets legally binding air quality limits for the protection of human health. The Government is committed to achieving full compliance with European air quality standards.

---

97 Appendix B of "The Civil Helicopter in the Community," British Helicopter Association: www.britishhelicopterassociation.org/?q=about-the-bha/guidelines

3.48   Our policy on air quality is to seek improved international standards to reduce emissions from aircraft and vehicles and to work with airports and local authorities as appropriate to improve air quality, including encouraging HGV, bus and taxi operators to replace or retrofit with pollution-reducing technology older, more polluting vehicles. There will be additional air quality (and noise pollution) benefits as the UK progresses to a low carbon economy with the likely increase in the proportion of electric vehicles and plug-in hybrid vehicles.

3.49   Around airports, sources of air pollution include aircraft engines, airport-related traffic on local roads and surface vehicles at the airport. The most important pollutants are oxides of nitrogen (NOx) and particulate matter (PM).

3.50   The Government assesses the UK's compliance with the EU air quality limits and target values. Air quality monitoring is also carried out by local authorities to support their local air quality management objectives. PM limits are largely met, but challenges remain with nitrogen dioxide, while pressures from increasing population, demands on transport and land use mean that considerable efforts to improve air quality to protect health and the environment continue to be needed. Air quality in local air quality management areas or where limit values are exceeded is particularly sensitive to new developments or transport pressures, and cumulative impacts from different individual sites can exacerbate this.

3.51   Studies have shown that NOx emissions from aviation-related operations reduce rapidly beyond the immediate area around the runway. Road traffic remains the main problem with regard to NOx in the UK. Airports are large generators of surface transport journeys and as such share a responsibility to minimise the air quality impact of these operations. The Government expects them to take this responsibility seriously and to work with the Government, its agencies and local authorities to improve air quality.

3.52   Whilst our policy is to give particular weight to the management and mitigation of noise in the immediate vicinity of airports, there may be instances where prioritising noise creates unacceptable costs in terms of local air pollution. For example, displacing the runway landing threshold to give noise benefits could lead to significant additional taxiing and emissions. For this reason, the impacts of any proposals which change noise or emissions levels should be carefully assessed to allow these costs and benefits to be weighed up.

3.53   As large sites which consume resources and emit waste, airports also have an impact on other aspects of the local environment such as water, waste management and habitat, through for example, de-icing of aircraft and runways, fuel handling and storage or the production of on-site heat or power. In England and Wales, where these activities produce waste, lead to discharges to local watercourses or groundwater, or are carried out using activities specified in the Environmental Permitting Regulations 2010, airports may require a permit from the Environment Agency or local authority. The permits contain conditions to protect the environment and human health, implement appropriate EU Directives and, where necessary, require the site operator to carry out monitoring.

3.54 Before taking decisions on any future new airport capacity, the Government will want to have a thorough understanding of the local environmental impacts of any proposals. As set out in its terms of reference, the Airports Commission's interim report will be informed by an initial high-level assessment of the credible long-term options which merit further detailed development. This will take into account local environmental factors, which are one of the broad categories which the Commission has identified in its recently published guidance document which scheme promoters should consider.[98] The Commission's final report will include an environmental assessment for each option, as well as consideration of their operational, commercial and technical viability.

3.55 It is likely that any proposals for any new hub airport or nationally significant infrastructure would be taken forward through an Airports National Policy Statement (NPS). This would take a similar approach to existing NPSs and be consistent with the Government's stated policies on sustainability and environmental protection. Loss of protected habitats, protected species, protected landscape and built heritage, and significant impacts on water resources and ecosystems would only be advocated if there were no feasible alternatives and the benefits of proposals clearly outweighed those impacts. Any unavoidable impacts would be mitigated or compensated for. Our policy will be to ensure there is full consideration of the environmental impacts of the most credible options for maintaining our international connectivity.

---

98 Guidance Document published 1 February 2012, at
    https://www.gov.uk/government/publications/submitting-evidence-and-proposals-to-the-airports-commission

4. Working together

The importance of local collaboration

4.1   Collaboration and transparency are important at every level: international, national and local. The focus of this chapter is on applying these principles more effectively at the local level, because we recognise that what happens around airports really matters to the communities who live and work there, and a national aviation policy can only be successful if it provides a sensible approach to addressing the concerns of communities.

4.2   There is currently a range of mechanisms for airports to engage with key stakeholders in the local area and beyond, including airport consultative committees (ACCs), airport master plans, airport transport forums (ATFs) and airport surface access strategies (ASASs). Responses to the consultation confirmed that there were many examples of good practice across the country where local stakeholders are working well together. Overall, existing mechanisms were seen as useful, but local community groups in particular felt there was room for improvement.

4.3   **Government's objective is to encourage the aviation industry and local stakeholders to strengthen and streamline the way in which they work together.** Local stakeholders have the experience and expertise to identify solutions tailored to their specific circumstances. We therefore want to encourage good practice rather than propose a 'one size fits all' model for local engagement.

4.4   However, there is scope to enhance the existing tools for local engagement with the aim of improving the quality of information produced, increasing the breadth of representation, avoiding duplication of activity and reducing the consultation burden on all concerned.

4.5   Airports, in partnership with local communities, should:

- take the opportunity to review the membership and terms of reference of their committees to ensure that local interests are fully represented and that there is no duplication of activity of committees;

- review their consultative timetables, for example for master plans and Noise Action Plans, with a view to aligning these where possible and reducing the consultative burden on all concerned;

- review the extent and detail of information that is published and set out clearly the methodology used. Airports should provide transparency and ensure that sufficient relevant information and opportunities for consultation reach a wide audience; and

- combine their ASASs into their published master plans to ensure a joined-up approach and make it easier for people to access information about the 'airport's plans.

Better arrangements for working together

Airport consultative committees (ACCs)

4.6   The Government expects all airports and aerodromes to communicate openly and effectively with their local communities about the impact of their operations. This aligns with policy set out in the National Planning Policy Framework that local authorities should work with neighbouring authorities to develop strategies for the provision of viable infrastructure necessary to support sustainable development, including transport investment necessary to support strategies for the growth of airports.

4.7   There are 51 airports and aerodromes in England, Wales and Scotland that have been designated[99] under section 35 of the Civil Aviation Act 1982 to provide adequate facilities for consultation with respect to any matter concerning the management or administration of the airport which affects the interests of users of the airport, local authorities and any other organisation representing the interests of persons concerned with the locality in which the airport is situated. However, the Government would not expect the absence of statutory designation to be a barrier to such consultation, as it should be a matter of good practice at airports of any size.

4.8   In practice ACCs carry out this role at the 51 designated airports and aerodromes. The work of ACCs should recognise the wider role of the airport as an important local employer and influential driver in the local economy, as well as considering the local environmental impacts of an airport, including noise. Their membership should reflect this balance of interests.[100] For example, ACCs may wish to work more closely with Local Enterprise Partnerships (LEPs) to support the needs of businesses and enterprise in their areas.

(working together)

---

99   SI 1996 No.1392 as amended by SI 2002 No. 2421

100 Membership of ACCs varies, but in line with the legislation will always include representatives from local authorities, local amenity groups (which may include residents' groups) and users of the airport (both airlines and passengers).

4.9   The Government would like to see ACCs play a more effective role, within their current statutory remit. In order to support ACCs in their work and to share best practice, we will review and update our 2003 guidance to ACCs. In doing so, we will retain the principle that this non-statutory guidance should remain flexible, proportionate and non-prescriptive and will want to ensure that we do not upset existing good governance and working arrangements. The review of guidance will also consider how the CAA might complement and support the work of ACCs through the use of its new functions in relation to publishing information about air transport services and about environmental matters (see paragraph 4.25).

4.10   Noise is the issue over which relations between airports and local communities have tended to break down. For this reason, the Government wants to see noise management marked by greater transparency, trust and local accountability of airports to local communities affected. Establishing good relations depends on local people feeling that engagement processes are effective, that noise impact data are credible and accessible and that the airport is honest about its local impacts and is willing to challenge its own performance. When updating the guidance, we will therefore look in particular at the scope for ACCs to play a stronger role in the noise management process, for example by monitoring implementation of airports' commitments made under statutory Noise Action Plans and being ready to challenge their performance.

Airport master plans

4.11   Currently over 30 airports across the UK have adopted master plans. They do not have a statutory basis, but the primary objective of master plans is to provide a clear statement of intent on the part of an airport operator to enable future development of the airport to be given due consideration in local planning processes. They also provide transparency and aid long-term planning for other businesses.

4.12   Government recommends that airports continue to produce master plans. We recommend that they are updated at least once every five years, and that the five-year periods should coincide where possible and appropriate with the periods covered by Noise Action Plans and airport surface access strategies, referred to below, to streamline the planning and engagement processes.

4.13   Government also recommends that airport operators consult on proposed changes to master plans, and engage more widely with local communities prior to publication, for example liaising more closely with local authorities and also through drop-in sessions and public meetings. Airport operators should notify the DfT or Devolved Administration when plans are revised, and highlight any material changes. Airport operators are also encouraged to advertise the publication of any revisions to their plans widely in their local area.

4.14 Research carried out by the DfT on the effectiveness of master plans has indicated that drafting for all audiences produces a tension between communicating future plans and providing a technical reference source. We therefore recommend that, where possible, the body of the document should be accessible to a lay person, and the technical detail clearly annexed.

4.15 Responses to the consultation showed the importance that stakeholders place on guidance, so a list of the content that the Government would recommend that airport operators include in the master plan is included at Annex B – though airports will wish to adopt their plans to suit local circumstances.

Airport transport forums

4.16 All airports in England and Wales with more than 1,000 passenger air transport movements a year are currently advised to set up air transport forums (ATFs). This concept was introduced in the previous administration's white paper *A New Deal for Transport: Better for Everyone*[101] and reiterated in the 2003 Air Transport White Paper.

4.17 The primary role of the forums is to serve local communities through:

- identifying short- and long-term targets for increasing the proportion of journeys made to airports by public transport;

- devising a strategy for meeting these targets; and

- overseeing implementation of the strategy.

4.18 The Government recognises the value of a continued partnership approach on surface access between airport operators, LEPs, local authorities, businesses, transport stakeholders and local communities. Airports may wish to retain the functions of ATFs, but should take the opportunity to review their membership and any opportunities for streamlining the work of ATFs with ACCs (notwithstanding the statutory obligations of ACCs) to ensure that forums are fully able to represent the needs of passengers, local employees and residents and freight.

4.19 General guidance is incorporated at Annex B.

Airport surface access strategies

4.20 Government attaches a high priority to effective public involvement in local transport policy. Local people, town and parish councils which have qualifying airports within their boundaries, business representatives, health and education providers, environmental and community groups should be involved in the development of airport surface access strategies. We

---

101 *A New Deal for Transport: Better for Everyone*, DfT, 1997, http://webarchive.nationalarchives.gov.uk/+/http:/www.dft.gov.uk/about/strategy/whitepapers/previous/anewdealfortransportbetterfo5695

recommend that ATFs produce airport surface access strategies (ASASs) to set out:

- targets for increasing the proportion of journeys made to the airport by public transport for both airport workers and passengers;

- the strategy to achieve those targets; and

- a system whereby the forum can oversee implementation of the strategy.

4.21 Timetables for updating ASASs were originally aligned with those for Local Transport Plans (LTPs). Although Local Transport Authorities do not now have to prepare a new LTP every five years, the statutory requirement to have and review an LTP remains and ASASs should take account of LTPs.

4.22 The Government recommends that airports continue to produce ASASs to set out targets for reducing the carbon and air quality impacts of surface access to airports, and to measure performance against these targets in a clear and transparent way. Airports may wish to consider whether there is any chance to reduce duplication of the functions and outputs of advisory groups.

4.23 The Government will work with the Airport Operators Association (AOA) and individual airports to continue to play an oversight role in surface access developments through carrying out the recommendations of the Low Carbon Transport to Airports project.[102] The South East Airport Taskforce (SEAT) recognised the value of the priorities for action agreed through the project:

- the DfT and AOA to continue to hold best practice forums on surface access;

- to provide better information to passengers; and

- to work with the National Business Travel Network to advise business travellers on low carbon travel options.

4.24 General guidance has been included at Annex B.

Improving information

4.25 Chapter 3 discusses how airports can improve their communications and provision of information to local communities about their local environmental impacts. The Civil Aviation Act 2012 gives the CAA a role in promoting better public information about the environmental effects of civil aviation in the UK, their impact on health and safety, and measures taken to mitigate adverse impacts. The CAA has also been given powers to produce guidance and advice for the industry with a view to reducing, controlling or mitigating the adverse effects of civil aviation in the UK. The new powers will be supported by a provision which enables the CAA to conduct or commission research in support of these functions.

---

102 *Low Carbon Transport to Airports Project Report*, DfT, July 2011, http://www.dft.gov.uk/publications/lcta-project-report

4.26 The Act also requires the CAA to consult on and publish a statement of policy on its exercise of these new functions, which will give the industry, interest groups and communities the opportunity to influence the use that the CAA makes of them. The CAA will shortly consult on its statement of policy. We expect that the CAA, in considering its new information functions, will have regard to how it can play an active role in ensuring airports publish environmental and wider performance-related information which is accessible (including to people living in the vicinity of the airport) and in a format which is useful to passengers when they make their choices.

5. Planning

Overview

5.1   This chapter explains the status of the Aviation Policy Framework and its interaction with existing planning guidance and policies and any decisions following the recommendations of the Airports Commission.

The status of the Aviation Policy Framework

5.2   The Aviation Policy Framework will apply to the whole UK and has been developed with input from the Devolved Administrations in Northern Ireland, Scotland and Wales. Aviation policy is largely a reserved matter, while planning and surface access policies are devolved. Some aspects of aviation noise policy are devolved but others are reserved. In so far as this Framework deals with matters which have been devolved it does so with the agreement of the administration in Belfast, Edinburgh and Cardiff as appropriate. Further details are set out in the separate section at the end of this chapter (see paragraph 5.25).

5.3   The Aviation Policy Framework, in conjunction with relevant policies and any decisions which Government may take in response to recommendations made by the Airports Commission, will fully replace the 2003 Air Transport White Paper and its associated guidance documents. Those documents are:

- *Guidance on the Preparation of Airport Master Plans* (DfT, July 2004)

- *Airport Transport Forums – Good Practice Guide* (DETR, April 2000)

- *Guidance on Airport Transport Forums and Airport Surface Access Strategies* (DETR, July 1999).

5.4   We will keep our policies under review and refresh them as needed; for example if there are major changes in the evidence supporting our policy objectives or in external circumstances. Any major changes will be subject to public consultation.

5.5   Should the Government decide to support any new nationally significant airport infrastructure following the conclusions of the Airports Commission's work, it is likely that the next step would be to draft and consult on a National Policy Statement for Airports. The Government has asked the Airports Commission to produce materials to support the Government in preparing a National Policy Statement to accelerate the resolution of any future planning application(s).

Planning policies

5.6 In preparing their local plans, local authorities are required to have regard to policies and advice issued by the Secretary of State. This includes the Aviation Policy Framework, to the extent it is relevant to a particular local authority area, along with other relevant planning policy and guidance. The Aviation Policy Framework may also be a material consideration in planning decisions depending on the circumstances of a particular application.

5.7 Paragraphs 3.19–3.22 in Chapter 3 explain how land-use planning and management is one of the elements of the ICAO balanced approach which should be explored when tackling noise problems at an airport.

Safeguarding

5.8 The National Planning Policy Framework (NPPF) makes clear that local planning authorities should 'identify and protect, where there is robust evidence, sites and routes which could be critical in developing infrastructure to widen choice'. This could apply to airport infrastructure.

5.9 Land outside existing airports that may be required for airport development in the future needs to be protected against incompatible development until the Government has established any relevant policies and proposals in response to the findings of the Airports Commission, which is due to report in summer 2015.

5.10 Airport operators to whom DfT Circular 01/2003 apply should maintain safeguarding maps to reflect potential proposals for future development of airports and ensure they are certified by the CAA.[103] This will ensure that the airport operator is consulted by the local planning authority over any planning applications which might conflict with safe operations at the airport, or nearby. The safeguarding map identifies areas by reference to the land height around the airport and its operational requirements, and describes the circumstances in which the local planning authority is required to consult the airport operator. The direction makes reference to the power of the Secretary of State to intervene where a local authority is minded to grant permission against the advice of the CAA.

103 Safeguarding aerodromes, technical sites and military explosive storage areas: The Town and County Planning (Safeguarding aerodromes, technical sites and military explosive storage areas) Direction 2002

Surface access

5.11 All proposals for airport development must be accompanied by clear surface access proposals which demonstrate how the airport will ensure easy and reliable access for passengers, increase the use of public transport by passengers to access the airport, and minimise congestion and other local impacts.

5.12 The general position for existing airports is that developers should pay the costs of upgrading or enhancing road, rail or other transport networks or services where there is a need to cope with additional passengers travelling to and from expanded or growing airports. Where the scheme has a wider range of beneficiaries, the Government will consider, along with other relevant stakeholders, the need for additional public funding on a case-by-case basis.

5.13 The Airports Commission has indicated that it will consider surface access needs as part of its work to assess options for maintaining the UK's international connectivity, in the context of existing and potentially new airports.

Public safety zones

5.14 Safety is a fundamental requirement for aviation, including at the local level. For people living and working near airports, safety is best assured by ensuring the safe operation of aircraft in flight. However, in areas where accidents are most likely to occur we seek to control the number of people at risk through the public safety zone (PSZ) system. PSZs are areas of land at the ends of runways at the busiest airports, within which development is restricted.

5.15 Our basic policy objective remains not to increase the number of people living, working or congregating in PSZs and, over time, to see the number reduced. Where necessary, we expect airport operators to offer to buy property which lies wholly or partly within those parts of the zones where the risk is greatest. We will continue to protect those living near airports by maintaining and, where justified, extending the PSZ system.

5.16 All of the above is contained in DfT Circular 01/2010, Control of Development in Airport Public Safety Zones.

Enterprise zones

5.17 The Government announced in Budget 2011 the creation of a number of enterprise zones in Local Enterprise Partnership (LEP) areas across England. Enterprise zones are geographically defined areas based around the core principle of reducing barriers for businesses to grow, with the intention of generating new businesses and jobs, through a combination of fiscal incentives and simplified planning controls. In England, 24 such zones have been established with the aim of driving local and national growth and contributing to the rebalancing of the economy.

5.18 As part of this initiative, an enterprise zone has been established around Manchester Airport. The proposed 'Airport City' is a £659 million, 150-acre development which will transform the airport into an international business destination and create up to 20,000 new jobs over the next 15 years. Manchester Airport is a key component of the Greater Manchester Strategy[104] and contributes £3.5 billion to the UK economy, providing direct employment to 26,000 people and supporting a further 50,000 jobs.[105]

5.19 To support further improvements to Greater Manchester's international connectivity and trade, a new Metrolink tramline is currently under construction that will connect the airport to the tram network which covers the city region. In addition, the Government announced in November 2012 that it would contribute £165 million to the A6 to Manchester Airport Link Road, which will connect the M56 and A6, improving access to the airport and enterprise zone.

5.20 An enterprise zone has also been established around Newquay airport, and the enterprise zone in Cardiff has been expanded to incorporate the airport. To recognise the importance of the airport to the wider Welsh economy, the First Minister of Wales formed the Cardiff Airport Task Force. The Task Force is a collaboration between the airport's owners, the Welsh Government and the wider public sector and business community. It will identify and recommend improvements and investments needed for Wales to boost air connectivity, improve the passenger experience and maximise its economic impact, commercially and for Wales. This is only one of many examples of good practice in this regard.

5.21 Early indications suggest that enterprise zones are proving successful in attracting interest from businesses and overseas investors, which should help to bolster growth at those airports. The Government, through UK Trade and Investment, is including enterprise zones in its strategic promotion of UK business and investment opportunities to potential overseas investors.

5.22 At other airports outside the South East, scope exists for LEPs to develop local strategies to maximise the catalytic effects of airports to attract business and support growth. LEPs, in partnership with local authorities, have a range of tools at their disposal to help support businesses in the vicinity of airports. There could also be scope for LEPs to take a more active role in feeding into airports' plans for surface access, to ensure that there is adequate public transport access for employees. The Government encourages airport operators to engage actively with their LEPs to ensure that they are fully integrated into their LEPs' overall economic strategy for the area, and to maximise the benefits to local economies.

---

104 *Greater Manchester Strategy*, 2011, http://neweconomymanchester.com/stories/842-greater_manchester_strategy
105 *Sustainability Report*, Manchester Airport Group, 2009/10, http://www.magworld.co.uk/sr2009/business/strategy.html

Reserved matters

5.23 The global nature of air transport requires the industry to operate in a complex network of international agreements, and in the UK's case, European legislation. Aviation policy and regulation in the UK is largely a reserved matter, which rests with the DfT and the Civil Aviation Authority (CAA). Reserved matters include safety regulation; economic regulation; aviation security; competition issues; and international aspects of aviation policy.

5.24 DfT has overall policy responsibility for UK aviation, and the CAA has UK-wide responsibilities for safety regulation, economic regulation, consumer protection and air traffic management. In addition, the Office of Fair Trading and the Secretary of State for Business, Innovation and Skills have a role under the Competition Act in relation to aviation competition issues.

Devolved matters

5.25 The role of the Devolved Administrations in relation to aviation is principally relevant to certain matters pertaining to land-use planning and airport surface access issues. Specifically:

a. The National Assembly for Wales has devolved powers relating to airports in terms of land-use planning and airport surface access issues.

b. The Scotland Act 1998 devolved responsibility for a number of areas of policy relevant to airports to the Scottish Executive. These include land-use planning; surface access policy; and responsibility for and funding of aerodromes in public ownership.

c. The Northern Ireland Act 1998 devolved responsibility for a number of areas of policy relevant to airports to the Northern Ireland Executive and Assembly. These include regional land-use planning; surface access policy and funding; and environmental policy. The Northern Ireland Executive also has responsibility for airport economic regulation; has powers over land in relation to aviation safety; the ability to grant aid for airport infrastructure; and may exercise certain controls relating to the management of airports.

Next steps

5.26 The Aviation Policy Framework sets out Government's high-level objectives and policy on aviation. As a framework, it brings together many related and discrete policies and work streams, some of which are in train. The next steps are:

a. In the summer of 2013 we will begin revising guidance to the CAA on its environmental objectives in respect of its air navigation functions, with the intention of issuing the guidance before the end of 2013.2013.

b. We will work with the CAA during 2013 to further develop the concept of noise envelopes, with the aim of producing guidance which can be used in the context of any proposals for new airport capacity and the work of the Airports Commission.

c. We will review guidance to Airport Consultative Committees later in 2013. This will update the existing 2003 guidance in the light of this new Policy Framework with the aim of supporting Committees in their work and sharing best practice.

d. Separately, the independent Airports Commission's important work of examining how best the UK can meet its international connectivity needs is well under way. The Commission will:

  i. Continue its public dialogue with further discussion papers on key issues, such as the economic value of a hub, to take into account as its work progresses.

  ii. By July 2013, have received outline proposals for any additional airport capacity in the long term (although the DfT would stress that it does not yet have a view on the case for additional capacity).

  iii. By the end of 2013, publish its interim report to Government and the opposition parties, setting out recommendations for immediate actions to improve the use of existing runway capacity in the short term. This should be consistent with credible long-term options which the Commission will be seeking to identify.

  iv. Publish its final report by Summer 2015.

Annex A: Noise controls

Table 1: Summary of noise control measures		
Control measure	**Set by**	**Enforcement/monitoring**
Aircraft noise certification limits	ICAO and the EU (UK Government contributes)	EASA/ the CAA.
Airspace use	Changes generally proposed by NATS/airports.	The CAA is responsible for the airspace change process, having regard to the Transport Act 2000, Air Navigation Directions and DfT guidance on environmental objectives.[106]
Noise Operational Controls – e.g.: • Noise-preferential routes • Night noise restrictions • Departure noise limits • Minimum height requirements after take-off • Continuous descent approach • Ground engine testing noise limits	Government (Heathrow, Gatwick and Stansted) Local authorities through local planning agreement Other airports have powers to make noise control schemes under the Civil Aviation Act 1982 as amended by Civil Aviation Act 2006.	Airports monitor compliance with controls by means of track-keeping and noise monitors Heathrow, Gatwick and Stansted compliance data reported to the DfT Reports to local authorities, local residents through Airport Consultative Committees (ACCs) and via Noise Action Plan reporting process.
Penalty schemes in relation to aircraft taking off or landing at the airport not complying with noise controls.	Airports The Government can require designated airports to have penalty schemes.	Airports Reports to local authorities, local residents through ACCs and via Noise Action Plan reporting process.
Fixing landing charges in relation to noise emissions	Airports The Government can direct designated and other airports to fix landing charges in relation to noise emissions.	Airports
Noise insulation grant schemes	Airports The Government can require grant schemes at designated airports.	Airports Reports to local authorities, local residents through ACCs and via Noise Action Plan reporting process.

106 Guidance to the CAA on Environmental Objectives Relating to the Exercise of its Air Navigation Functions

Annex B: Guidance on master plans, airport transport forums and airport surface access strategies

This Annex replaces existing guidance on the content of airport master plans, ATFs and ASASs.

Master plans

Suggested content

B.1   The Government recommends that the more ground covered in a master plan and the more extensive the consultation which has informed its preparation, the greater its value in informing future land use, transport and economic planning processes, and in supporting prospective planning applications. We would anticipate that, in the case of most airports, master plans will address the following 'core' areas:

- forecasts;

- infrastructure proposals;

- safeguarding and land/property take (please see paragraph B.5);

- impact on people and the natural environment; and

- proposals to minimise and mitigate impacts.

Forecasts

B.2   It would be helpful for airport operators to provide an introduction to the forecasts on which the master plan is based in the form of an up-to-date breakdown of current traffic (daytime and night-time, passenger, cargo and air transport movements). An explanation of this data in relation to historic trends and expected market developments would provide important context.

Infrastructure proposals

B.3   To help recipients of the master plan it would be helpful for airports to include information on existing airside and terminal infrastructure. It may also be helpful if airports were to include a statement of their adopted planning standards. These would include issues such as gate utilisation and queue lengths for normal throughput, average and maximum delay criteria for landings and take-offs and how these would impact on their proposals.

B.4   The plans are not expected to take the form of detailed engineering or architectural drawings, such as those that might accompany a planning application, but to be of value they ought to contain sufficient information, including drawings where appropriate, so that they may be clearly understood by the lay person as well as professionals. In addition to airside and terminal development and surface access infrastructure, plans for the next ten years might usefully include landside development (e.g. car parking, servicing and support areas, environmental features, landscaping and other mitigation measures), clearly identifying what is new and what already exists. They should also show airport boundaries and highlight any additional properties or land that may need to be taken. Maps showing safety surfaces and PSZs can be provided separately (see below).

Safeguarding and land/property take

B.5   Perhaps one of the most important issues master plans should seek to address is what the long-term land requirements are for future airport development and whether this requires changes to airport boundaries. Where it does, the additional land and property involved, including those associated with PSZs and safety surfaces, should be clearly identified to minimise long-term uncertainty and non-statutory blight.

Mitigation

B.6   Proposals for mitigation measures across the major impact areas identified will be an important component of master plans; for example emission controls, noise abatement measures, sound insulation, surface access schemes and traffic management and measures to address landscape and biodiversity impacts.

B.7   It will be appropriate for master plans to address any proposals for compensation measures that may be required where the scale of impacts is such that they cannot adequately be mitigated. Such measures might include appropriate voluntary purchase schemes and assistance with relocation costs where the extent of property and land-take is clear.

Airport transport forums

Suggested content

B.8   The Government suggests that ATFs are made up of the following groups:

- Airport operator (who should lead the forum);
- Local Highway Authority and Integrated Transport Authority;
- Local Enterprise Partnership;

- Local transport providers (e.g. bus, rail, coach, car hire);

- Local authorities;

- Passenger representatives;

- Freight industry representatives;

- Local businesses;

- Representative from the Airport Consultative Committee;

- Representatives of airport users;

- Representatives of airport employees; and

- Bodies representing interests of walkers, cyclists and disabled people in the area.

B.9 However, the Government recognises that local circumstances will have a bearing on the make-up of the group. This list should not therefore be taken to be prescriptive or exhaustive.

B.10 The Government suggests that ATFs should meet at least twice per year, and engage proactively in dialogue with group members throughout the year.

B.11 In order to ensure the forum is effective, we recommend that airport operators should limit the membership to a manageable number. However they should engage frequently in wider consultation with interested parties including members of the local community e.g. through workshops.

B.12 Costs relating to ATFs should be borne by the airport operator.

Airport surface access strategies

Suggested content

B.13 The Government suggests that ASASs should include:

- analysis of existing surface access arrangements;

- targets for increasing the proportion of journeys made to the airport by public transport by passengers and employees; cycling and walking. There should be short- and long-term targets;

- consideration of whether freight road traffic can be reduced;

- consideration of how low carbon alternatives could be employed;

- short-term actions and longer-term proposals and policy measures to deliver on targets such as:

- proposed infrastructure developments e.g. light rail;

- car/taxi sharing schemes;

- improved information provision on public transport, cycling and walking options;

- car park management; and

- through-ticketing schemes;

- indication of the cost of any proposals;

- performance indicators for delivering on targets;

- monitoring and assessment strategies (internal and external); and

- green transport incentive schemes for employees.

B.14 The Government recognises that different targets and proposals for meeting targets will be appropriate for different areas. This list is therefore not prescriptive or exhaustive.

Annex C: Glossary

ACC	Airport Consultative Committees
AGP	Aerospace Growth Partnership
ANMAC	Aircraft Noise Management Advisory Committee
APFG	Airport Performance Facilitation Group
AOA	Airport Operators Association
ASC	Adaption Sub-Committee
ASASs	Airport Surface Access Strategies
ATF	Airport Transport Forums
ATOL	Air Travel Organisers Licensing
ATT	Alternatives to travel
BIS	Department for Business, Innovation and Skills
BRIC	Brazil, Russia, India and China
CAA	Civil Aviation Authority
CAEP	Committee on Aviation Environmental Protection
CBP	Customs and Border Protection
CCC	Committee on Climate Change
CCRA	Climate change risk assessment
CDA	continuous descent approach
CO_2	carbon dioxide
DECC	Department of Energy and Climate Change
DfT	Department for Transport
DOH	Department for Health
EASA	European Aviation Safety Agency
EU	European Union
ETS	Emissions Trading System

FAB	functional airspace blocks
FABEC	FAB Europe Central
FAS	Future Airspace Strategy
GA	general and business aviation
GDP	gross domestic product
GHG	greenhouse gas
GVA	gross value added
HAL	Heathrow Airport Limited
HS2	High Speed 2
IATA	International Air Transport Association
ICAO	International Civil Aviation Organization
ILUC	indirect land use change
IRIS	iris recognition immigration system
LEP	Local Enterprise Partnership
LTP	Local Transport Plans
Mt CO_2	million tonnes of CO_2
NAP	National Adaption Programme
NATS	(formerly National Air Traffic Services)
NOx	nitrogen oxides
NPPF	National Planning Policy Statement
NPRs	noise-preferential routes
NPS	National Policy Statement
OBR	Office for Budget Responsibility
OECD	Organisation for Economic Co-operation and Development
PM	particulate matter
PSOs	Public Service Obligations
PSZ	public safety zones
PwC	Pricewaterhouse Coopers
RDFs	Route Development Funds
SEAT	South East Airports Taskforce
SES	Single European Sky
SOx	sulphur oxides
UAVs	unmanned aerial vehicles
WWF	World Wildlife Fund